W9-CJX-494

JX
1946
P4

Peace projects of the eighteenth century:
comprising A shorter project for perpetual peace [by] Charles [Castel] de
Saint-Pierre, Abbé de Tiron; A project
of perpetual peace [by] Jean-Jacques
Rousseau [and] Plan for an universal
and perpetual peace [by] Jeremy Bentham.
With a new introduction for the Garland
edition by M. C. Jacob.   New York,
Garland Publishing, 1974.
1 v. (various pagings) (The Garland

(continued next card)

The
Garland Library
of
War and Peace

The
Garland Library
of
War and Peace

Under the General Editorship of

Blanche Wiesen Cook, *John Jay College, C.U.N.Y.*

Sandi E. Cooper, *Richmond College, C.U.N.Y.*

Charles Chatfield, *Wittenberg University*

Peace Projects
of the Eighteenth Century

comprising

A Shorter Project for Perpetual Peace

**Charles [Castel] de Saint-Pierre,
Abbé de Tiron**

A Project of Perpetual Peace

Jean-Jacques Rousseau

Plan for an Universal and Perpetual Peace

Jeremy Bentham

with a new introduction
for the Garland Edition by

M. C. Jacob

Garland Publishing, Inc., New York & London
1974

The new introduction for this

Garland Library Edition is Copyright © 1974, by

Garland Publishing Inc.

Library of Congress Cataloging in Publication Data
Main entry under title:

Peace projects of the eighteenth century.

(The Garland library of war and peace)
Reprint of the 1927 ed. of Saint-Pierre's Selections
from the second edition of the Abrégé du projet de paix
perpétuelle, published by Sweet and Maxwell, London,
which was issued as no. 5 of Grotius Society publications; of the translation of Extrait du projet de paix
perpétuelle de Monsieur l'abbé de Saint-Pierre, par
J. J. Rousseau, published in 1927 by R. Cobden-
Sanderson, London; and of the 1939 ed. of Bentham: plan
for an universal and perpetual peace, being selections
from his Principles of international law, published by
Peace Book Co., London, which was issued as no. 6 of
Peace classics.
    1. Peace. I. Saint-Pierre, Charles Irénée Castel,
abbé de, 1658-1743. Abrégé du projet de paix
perpétuelle. English. Selections. 1974. II. Saint-
Pierre, Charles Irénée Castel, abbé de, 1658-1743.
Extrait du projet de paix perpétuelle. English. 1974.
III. Bentham, Jeremy, 1748-1832. Principles of
international law. Selections. 1974. IV. Series.
V. Series: Grotius Society. Publications, no. 5.
JX1946.P4   327'.172   78-147421
ISBN 0-8240-0215-6

Printed in the United States of America

Introduction

As Kant remarked, the eighteenth century was not an enlightened age. The aims of governments, the dictates of commercial and colonial expansion, and the desire for European dominance remained motives for war, just as they had been in centuries past. The necessity remained for those who would institute peace to formulate projects and theories by which it might be secured. But unlike their predecessors in this search, eighteenth-century theoreticians could see themselves as part of a larger intellectual project, a European-wide attempt to develop principles of social and human behavior which would, if applied, usher in an age of Enlightenment. The three thinkers presented in this volume, Saint-Pierre, Rousseau, and Bentham, represent various stages in the search for Enlightenment, and their proposals in turn reflect interesting and often unnoticed aspects of eighteenth-century thought.

The Abbé de Saint-Pierre (b. 1658) belongs to that crucial period from 1680 to 1720 when the philosophical and political currents of the seventeenth century were redefined and assimilated to produce the foundations upon which Enlightenment thought would rest.[1] Saint-Pierre's peace proposals evolve out of his personal dialogue with Hobbes and Descartes,[2]

5

and out of his consequent desire to find a formula by which Leviathan and its rulers would systematically and mechanically divorce their interests from the war-making process. The Abbé conceived the state as a Cartesian mechanism, and in turn he desired to find for it principles by which its operation could be analyzed and subjected to the dictates of reason. Mixed with his Cartesianism, and saving him from its excesses, there is also a dedication to practicality and utility, and this further places Saint-Pierre in the tradition of French utilitarianism[3] that emerged in the late seventeenth century, often in opposition to the baroque and scholastic arguments used to bolster the absolutist claims of both church and state.

In keeping with Hobbes' notion of the sovereign, Saint-Pierre envisioned a confederation of rulers whose absolute power to maintain domestic peace would now be extended, and yet constrained, to produce an international peace. All would subject their will to dictates of the confederation, and much of Saint-Pierre's argument centers on his attempt to prove that peace serves self-interest. Peace is useful, it costs less and produces stability. Furthermore, a confederation of princes would come to the aid of a member against any uprising or rebellion within his country.[4] Saint-Pierre would bolster the power of monarchy in order to secure international peace. He imagined that the prospect of the former would entice European monarchs into accepting the latter.

What Saint-Pierre never understood, and the same

6

can be said of Bentham, was the economic advantages gained out of the process of war. Each of these theoreticians of Enlightenment in one way or another fail, understandably, to realize the importance of financial gain, whether obtained through the conquest of colonies or through the expenditure of state revenues in the financing of a war machine. In the absence of a science of economics, Saint-Pierre dwells upon human psychology, and he defines power almost solely in political terms. In this definition the imprint of seventeenth-century theories is most clearly evident in his thought.

Saint-Pierre's appeal to the power instincts of monarchy also grew out of his concrete experience as a court minister and as a participant in the negotiations that produced the Treaty of Utrecht (1713). That his scheme for peace met with no success in its own time and that he eventually became an object of suspicion in court circles tells us far more about the nature of the ancien régime than it does about whatever weaknesses we may discern in the Abbé's conception of human motivation and the necessities of state.

Saint-Pierre's place as a transitional figure in the intellectual history of Europe finds added confirmation in the impact his theories had on the young Rousseau, for his Project of Perpetual Peace, reprinted in this volume, was closely modeled on Saint-Pierre's. And Rousseau scholars have either noted that fact, with the added caveat that Rousseau

condescendingly regarded the Abbé as an impractical man,[5] or more interestingly, they have generally ignored Rousseau's writings on peace. They have done so because, like certain of his other treatises, Rousseau's project does not fit neatly or tidily into his more general theories about natural man, the general will, and the social contract.

Encouraged by the deceased Abbé's friends, Rousseau examined a large collection of his notes and papers between 1754 and 1756 for the purpose of editing his writings. Rousseau found Saint-Pierre's prose awkward and dull, and decided to write a modernized version of the Project. At least one student of Saint-Pierre has argued that the young Rousseau derived many of his mature ideas from his careful study of the Abbé's writings.[6] Although in some instances the arguments advanced for that claim appear less than convincing,[7] they need not concern us here. What must be done is to decide how Rousseau's treatise on peace relates to his other writings.

Rousseau, perhaps more than any other modern political theorist, has generated enormous scholarly controversy simply because he sometimes appears to be contradictory.[8] His writings on war and peace are at times obviously consistent with his later thought. For instance, he has little use for Hobbes' pessimistic assessment of man's natural warlike condition, and he sees war as the almost inevitable by-product of selfish economic motives embodied in the very nature of

society and reflected in the policies of the modern state.[9] All that saves men from total destruction is what remains of their natural sentiments for harmony and compassion, for man in society is tortured and in turn he tortures through the mechanisms of war making. The modern state and its monarchs, as Rousseau sees them, exercise their most pernicious tendencies when they engage in war, and he would stop them by instituting the confederation first proposed by Saint-Pierre.

Yet in the very taking up of the Abbé's proposal Rousseau appears to be at war with his own principles. Princes, he argues, would enhance their power through such a union; revolutions would have little chance of success. The Abbé's proposal, if adopted, would, it seems, undermine the social and human transformations that Rousseau so passionately advocated.

Why then would Rousseau espouse a proposal seemingly at variance with his most treasured principles? To answer that question I would ask the reader to think briefly about another of Rousseau's often neglected treatises, The Government of Poland. *There too Rousseau prescribes a set of practical principles for the establishment of a Polish constitution which his commentators have often seen as contradictory to his theoretical and general writings.[10] I would suggest that in both instances Rousseau merely recognizes that his general principles for the reform of existing societies bear little rele-*

vance to his age, and that any concrete reforms, if they have any hope of success, must address themselves to the status quo. *Rousseau, as a proud man, had no intention of being dismissed as absurd or impractical, and therefore when he addressed himself to the immediate problems of war and peace, or of constitutional monarchy, he holds his principles aside, revealing them only indirectly, and concentrates on the business at hand. Nonetheless his fierce denunciation of greed as one of the main causes of war, and his passionate plea for peace as essential to human happiness, both rendered in highly emotional terms in* A Project, *tell us that the practical Rousseau has merely concealed, but not for an instance abandoned, his hatred for existing governments and their rulers. Rousseau, like Saint-Pierre, failed to have his peace proposal adopted, but it is doubtful that Rousseau's failure caused him the least surprise.*

Perhaps a comparable realism influenced Bentham when he failed to have published in his lifetime his own Plan for a Universal and Perpetual Peace. *This treatise, a part of his* Principles of International Law, *bears no exact date of composition – it was probably written sometime between 1786 and 1789 – and there is no way of knowing how accurately it portrays Bentham's understanding of the process by which Europeans might secure peace. Certainly the* Plan *conforms to the general principles articulated by Bentham and on which his fame as a political theorist rests.*

INTRODUCTION

Bentham's treatise, like those of Saint-Pierre and Rousseau, reveals aspects of his thought and, therefore, of the Enlightenment, which generally go unmentioned. In Saint-Pierre's we find a clear example of the philosopher's debt to seventeenth-century theories; in Rousseau's project we may find an excellent example of the philosopher as a practical statesman. In Bentham's plan what stands out most noticeably is his total disregard for the necessities of capitalistic economics. Bentham's utilitarianism, summarized by the maxim "the greatest good for the greatest number," rested not on a glorification of selfishness and self-interest,[11] but rather on Bentham's profound moral indignation. True to his age he desired to reform existing political institutions and bring them into conformity with the needs of the majority of the society. His emphasis on pleasure seeking and the concomitant avoidance of pain leads Bentham into the presumption that peace is an obvious goal desired by all mankind. As a lawyer and a theorist of jurisprudence Bentham would establish a European court with the power to enforce peace and punish its violators.

Yet if peace is so obviously the greatest good, why do men wage war? Bentham would lay blame on the search for, and the maintenance of, colonies. Thus the burden of his remarks rests on proving that colonies are a waste of time and money. Capital, as Bentham understands it, is fixed and can be invested in any number of enterprises with the same results.

11

INTRODUCTION

So, he argues, why not invest the capital elsewhere, obtain equal profit, and simultaneously eliminate one of the main causes of European wars?

Bentham failed to understand the nature of capitalistic and commercial expansion and the absolute necessity of foreign markets and colonial resources. His utilitarian psychology, lacking a grounding in the concrete necessities of government, founders when he attempts its application to the problems of war and peace. Of the three treatises reprinted, Bentham's strikes the modern reader as the most naive. Perhaps Bentham also came to see its failings and for that reason never published it. We read it today less for what it tells us about a means for the maintenance of peace, and more for what it tells us about the shortcomings of the Enlightenment.

Yet the ideals of the Enlightenment would have been shallow and incomplete had not at least a few of its major spokesmen bothered not simply to decry war, as did Voltaire, but also to formulate concrete proposals for the establishment of peace. With this reprinting of those proposals the philosophes once again address themselves to an unenlightened age.

M. C. Jacob
Baruch College — C.U.N.Y.

12

NOTES

[1] *See Paul Hazard*, The European Mind, 1680-1715 *(New York, 1967)*.

[2] *Merle L. Perkins*, The Moral and Political Philosophy of the Abbé de Saint-Pierre *(Paris, 1959), pp. 87-95*.

[3] *L. Rothkrug*, Opposition to Louis XIV: The Political and Social Origins of the French Enlightenment *(Princeton, 1965), pp. 315-28, 465*.

[4] *C. I. Castel de Saint-Pierre*, Abrégé du Projet de Paix Perpétuelle *(Garland reprint, 1974), p. 35*.

[5] *See F. C. Green*, Jean-Jacques Rousseau *(Cambridge, 1955), p. 282*.

[6] *Merle L. Perkins, op. cit., pp. 106-07*.

[7] Ibid, *especially p. 118*.

[8] *A good summary of current Rousseau scholarship appears in Peter Gay*, The Party of Humanity *(New York, 1964)*.

[9] *Mario Einaudi*, The Early Rousseau *(Ithaca, N.Y., 1967), pp. 208-23*.

[10] *This problem receives excellent treatment in Willmore Kendall's introduction to* The Government of Poland *(New York, 1972)*.

[11] *A point aptly demonstrated in M. P. Mack*, Jeremy Bentham: An Odyssey of Ideas *(New York, 1963)*.

13

THE GROTIUS SOCIETY PUBLICATIONS.

Texts for Students of International Relations.

No. 5.

Selections

from the second edition of the

Abrégé du Projet de Paix Perpétuelle.

BY

C. I. CASTEL DE SAINT-PIERRE, Abbot of Tiron.

1738.

Translated by H. HALE BELLOT, M.A.

WITH AN INTRODUCTION

BY

PAUL COLLINET,

Professor of Law in the University of Paris.

SWEET & MAXWELL, LIMITED,

2 & 3 CHANCERY LANE, LONDON, W.C. 2.

1927.

(Printed in England.)

PRINTED IN GREAT BRITAIN BY
THE EASTERN PRESS, LTD., READING.

INTRODUCTION.

CHARLES FRANÇOIS IRENÉE CASTEL DE SAINT-PIERRE, born on February 13, 1658, at the *château* of Saint-Pierre-Église, between Cherbourg and Barfleur, the eighth of the thirteen children of a *Grand Bailli* of the Cotentin, related to the Marshal Villars and to the Marshal Bellefonds, studied theology at Caen, and established himself in Paris in a small house in the Faubourg Saint-Jacques in 1680, there to lead the unfettered life of a student. Natural science and medicine first caught his interest, to be followed by moral and political philosophy. He " sought after great men." He frequented the *salons*. He called upon La Bruyère, who, annoyed by his passion for argument, made fun of him in his *Caractères* under the name of *Mopse* (1690). He was easy to caricature. A man with the courage of his convictions, and sure of their soundness, he was careless to conceal his self-esteem, " shameless and unabashed."

The Abbé arrived in Paris with works on the reform of government and the reduction of the volume of litigation either already written or at the back of his mind. The better to obtain an insight into the court, he bought, about 1688, the office of first almoner to Madame, Duchess of Orleans, the celebrated Princess Palatine, mother of the Regent, a post which he resigned some time before 1711. The friendship of Fontenelle and the interest of Madame de Lambert, who kept one of the best known of the *salons*, procured him in 1694 the entry to the French Academy, although he had as yet published none of his political studies.

He became commendatory abbot of Tiron in 1702.

In January, 1712, the Abbé de Saint-Pierre was chosen as his secretary by the abbé and future cardinal, Polignac, one of the three plenipotentiaries of France at the conference at Utrecht, which was destined to end the war of the Spanish Succession. He had then already written the first draft of the work on an Everlasting Peace, which was to make him famous, and from which are taken the selections which follow. But neither the public nor Louis XIV. yet knew of the work; a

privileged few, the Duchess of Orleans, and the Duke of Burgundy, the hope of the reformers, alone had read it in manuscript. The book, which I shall discuss below in more detail, was printed during the conference at Utrecht itself, in 1713, under the title of *Projet de paix perpétuelle.*

The Abbé remained in Holland for over a year. The stay had a great influence upon his political ideas, and enabled him to study commerce and banking, the ground-work of that economic system which was the precursor of the utilitarianism of Bentham.

On his return from Holland in 1713, still living in the apartments of the Duchess of Orleans in the Palais Royal, where he stayed until after 1739, he published between 1714 and 1718 a number of *mémoires*, particularly that on the *Taille Tarifée*, in which he recommended a graduated income tax in place of the arbitrary *taille* then in force. He became more and more, as he put it, "counsel for the commonweal." But in spite of the change of system after the death of Louis XIV., his too bold opinions met with no success. On the contrary, Cardinal Polignac, himself formerly his patron, caused him to be excluded, in 1718, from the Academy for having disparaged the memory of the great King in his famous *Discours sur la Polysynodie* (or multiplicity of Councils), the best of his studies on domestic politics, as the *Projet de paix perpétuelle* is the best on international law.

Although then sixty years old the Abbé did not go into retirement. He found in private society at the *Entresol*, which was organised after 1720 after the fashion of the English clubs, and became the parent of the *Academie des sciences morales et politiques*, willing auditors whom he deluged with innumerable projects of the most diverse kind designed to render society "perfect":—statistics, administration, education, medicine, the peerage, war, navigation, finance, diplomacy, ethics, the drama, preaching. He recommended institutions which have only been set up in our own day—schools for girls, an Academy of Medicine, a *Banque de France*, a Prize Court—or which have not yet been and perhaps never will be realised—the abolition of pauperism, the marriage of Catholic priests, spelling reform, the election of officials, &c. He invented a machine to provide exercise indoors, the "*tremoussoir.*" He coined words, two of which

have survived him, " bienfaisance " (beneficence) and " gloriole " (vainglory).

These bold schemes, which caused him to be regarded by the first minister, Fleury, as a " tiresome and disturbing agitator," caused the closure of the *Entresol* in 1731. The Abbé de Saint-Pierre continued his propaganda in the *salons* of Madame de Tencin, Madame Geoffrin and Madame Dupin, the grandmother of Georges Sand. He was, according to Rousseau, the " spoilt child " of the fine ladies of the time, although, on his own avowal, his talk was not as good as his ideas. From this period date the sixteen duodecimo volumes of the *Ouvrages de Politique et de Morale* (1733—1741).

Leaving unpublished his *Annales politiques* (a), he ended his laborious life full of hope on April 29, 1743, at the age of eighty-five, at 16 Faubourg Saint-Honoré.

The Abbé de Saint-Pierre, in spite of vexations, in spite of the defeat of his plans of reform, remained, in fact, all his life an optimist. He trusted to the prevalence of reason, while proclaiming that men were but children, and kings still more childish. Rousseau summed him up : " He would have been a very wise man had he not been so absurdly reasonable." One of his biographers, Goumy, has called him the patriarch of the " Philosophes," for with his bold ideas he was the forerunner of the writers known by that name who prepared men's minds for the French Revolution of 1789. But he had over them the advantage, due doubtless to his Norman origin, of possessing the sense of " utility," of what was practicable. In his own words, he wished to make government " much more honourable for the king, much more convenient for ministers, and much more useful to the people." Yet in his own days, and since, he has been regarded as a dreamer.

THE PROJET DE PAIX PERPETUELLE.

The peculiar importance of the text printed.

The Abbé de Saint-Pierre had by 1707 sketched out his idea for securing everlasting peace and had already begun to elabor-

(a) Published after his death, and re-edited by Joseph Drouet, Paris 8, 55.

them before 1711 (b). The work in its first published form was
printed at Cologne in 1712 under the title of *Mémoire pour rendre
la paix perpétuelle en Europe*; in its final form it appeared at
Utrecht in 1713 under the title of *Projet pour rendre la paix
perpétuelle en Europe*, 2 vol.; it was completed in 1717 by the
issue of a third volume *Le Projet de traité pour rendre la paix
perpétuelle entre souverains chrétiens*.

An *Abrégé du Projet de paix perpétuelle* was published by the
author in 1729, of which there appeared a new edition in 1738.

The *Projet* consists of five fundamental articles of which we
shall give a summary, omitting for the sake of clarity the complicated and tedious details (c).

First, after a Preface, the author gives the reasons for which
the Christian Powers of Europe should sign these five articles,
by adding up under nine headings the advantages which they
would derive from the signature of an everlasting peace, both
international and domestic—security, economies, growth of commerce, general welfare (d).

To secure a permanent peace the twenty-four Christian States
of Europe, maintained within the frontiers assigned to them by
the Treaty of Utrecht, are to form among themselves a Grand
Alliance or European Union. The twenty-four States are each
to nominate a delegate, two substitutes, and two agents to take
the places of the substitutes. Large and small States are to
have equal representation. The twenty-four delegates or plenipotentiaries are to constitute the Senate of Peace, which is to
sit permanently at Utrecht. The President is to be the Prince
of Peace. To secure the independence of the Senate he is to
change each week.

(b) *Correspondence de Madame, Duchesse d'Orleans* . . . Ranke et Holland,
traduction Jaeglé, 12mo, Paris, 1880, II., p. 86 : " Marly, 28 June, 1711 (to
the Duchess of Hanover), . . . you and I are among the brotherhood of
peace-loving folk as much as the Abbé de Saint-Pierre, who is now my first
almoner. He draws up project upon project for securing everlasting peace.
He wants to write a whole book upon it. Here are his first sheets; but I
doubt if he completes the work; people are already making fun of it. . . ."

(c) The extracts which follow are taken from the *Abrégé*. They differ
in some respects from the text of the *Projet*. We have deemed it best to
unmarise here the original scheme of the author, according to the *Projet*.
^ reader will thus be enabled to trace the development of the volatile ideas
mind always in a state of effervescence.

Infra, pp. 24-5, 53-4.

Such is Article I. (*e*).

Article II. relates to the revenue necessary to the support of an international army (See Article IV.), to the payment of the plenipotentiaries and resident Ministers, and to the organisation, until an Asiatic Union is also established, of the defence of the frontiers of the European Union against invasion from the East. The contribution of each State is to be determined monthly by the delegates of the Grand Alliance, and is to be in proportion to the revenue and charges of the States. It is to be a European Month after the pattern of the Roman Month of the Holy Roman Empire (*f*).

Article III. is the most important and amounts to this:—

In case of dispute between two States, the States in disagreement must first seek reconciliation through the *obligatory mediation* of the rest of the members of the Grand Alliance. In event of the failure of mediation, an award or *arbitration* becomes necessary. It is to be rendered by the Senate of Peace, which thus becomes, above all, a tribunal, a permanent and compulsory Court of Arbitration. The award is to be made first, provisionally, by a plurality of votes. The definitive award is only to be made five years later and must be adopted by a majority of three-fourths: the caution of the author is to be observed (*g*).

How is the award to be executed? The author answers, in Article IV., " by force." What force? He perceives that the Powers will in a time of peace only maintain weak forces for the preservation of civil order: that is what is meant by disarmament, a source of economy. If it should be necessary to proceed against one of the Powers which refuses to submit to an award or to regulations made by the Grand Alliance, or enters into treaties incompatible with it, or makes preparations for war (precluded in theory by supervision by representatives resident in each State), each State must furnish a contingent of special troops, which shall be placed under a generalissimo, appointed by the Senate of Peace, and having no existence in normal times —a further measure of prudence. The author postulates the maintenance of existing treaties concluded since the Treaty of Westphalia; he recognises the right to negotiate fresh treaties.

(*e*) *Infra*, pp. 24-6, 53. (*f*) *Infra*, pp. 26-7, 54-5. (*g*) *Infra*, pp. 27-8, 55.

But he desires to abolish secret diplomacy. Exchange of territory and treaties between sovereigns are to be concluded with
the consent of, and under the guarantee of, the Union, acting
by a three-fourths majority (h).

Finally, Article V. provides for the modification of agreements.
A plurality of votes is sufficient for the regulation of all those
matters required to give the greatest possible strength, security,
and other advantages to the Grand Alliance; but nothing is to
be changed in the five fundamental articles without the unanimous consent of all the Allies (i).

In a second section he points out to the sovereigns, first the
Emperor, then the King of France, then to the other rulers of
Europe, the powerful motives which they have for signing the
articles.

The third section comprises the objections to his scheme and
the refutation of them.

It is sufficient to read this summary to realise its importance.
But before insisting upon that let us observe what is the relation
of the *Projet* to previous schemes.

Its relation to previous thought.

The first work upon the establishment of an everlasting peace
is, as is well known, the *Nouveau Cynée* of Eméric Crucé
(1623) (k). The Abbé de Saint-Pierre did not know of it; it was
Leibnitz who pointed it out to him. The *Nouveau Cynée,* moreover, was limited to the advocacy of the institution of a council
of arbitration with the disfavour of other princes as its sole
sanction. This was also Grotius's conception.

On the other hand the Abbé had read the summary of the
Œconomies royales of Sully which is given by *Péréfixe*, where
the Grand Design of Henry IV. (l) is frequently quoted, of which
the author was the minister himself and not the king.

The Grand Design is the foundation of the work of the Abbé

(h) *Infra*, pp. 28-9, 55-6.
(i) *Infra*, pp. 29-30, 56.
(k) The best study of this work is that by M. Pierre Louis Lucas, *Un
plan de paix et de liberté du commerce au XVII siècle; Le Nouveau Cynée
d'Eméric Crucé* (1623), Paris, 1919.
(l) A translation of this work forms No. 2 of this Series.

de Saint-Pierre, who had the shrewdness to shelter himself un
the popular name of Henry IV., and presented his scheme a
mere elucidation of the work attributed to the king (m).
connection between his book and the Grand Design is explicit in
the title of the third volume of the *Projet* (1717), as well as in
that of the *Abrégé* (1729), as will be noticed in the Bibliography
(p. 11, *infra*). But in reality he did better than elucidate the
Grand Design. That offered, in opposition to the pretensions of
the House of Austria to universal monarchy, a republic of
Christian States. The Abbé carried the idea further, developed
it, and transformed it by his familiar method of a formal proof
like that employed in geometry (which has contributed not a little
to make his books unreadable). He supported it with numerous
arguments, he formulated the objections which had been made
to it, and he tried to refute them. In place of confining himself,
like his predecessors, to generalities, he had the merit of drawing
up practical regulations for the establishment of a European
Diet (n). He excelled his model in that his work was more
broadly planned, more firmly knit, more precise in detail, than
any other which had come before it and than those of Bentham
and Kant which were to come after.

Yet there have not, either in the past or in our own days,
lacked critics of the *Projet de paix perpétuelle*.

The criticism and subsequent modification of the doctrine contained in the Projet.

The plan so forcibly set out by the Abbé de Saint-Pierre was
too far in advance of the opinion of his time to meet with complete approval from the scholars and princes of Europe to whom
his book was addressed. Madame, Duchess of Orleans, wrote,
before the book had appeared, that fun was already being made
of him. In 1715 Liebnitz confessed to Grimarest his private
opinion of the *Projet*, which he thought utopian, in terms still
worth attention to-day: " I have seen something of the plan of

---

(m) See the Introduction by David Ogg to *Texts for Students of International Relations*, (No. 2), p. 9.
(n) J. Drouet, *L'Abbé de Saint-Pierre. L'homme et l'œuvre*, p. 123.

de Saint-Pierre for the maintenance of an everlasting peace
Europe. It reminds me of a motto on a grave, *pax perpetua;*
the dead fight not; but the living are of another temper, and
the most powerful have little respect for courts '' (o).

Although, to make his work more readable, the author had
condensed it in an *Abrégé*, he met no better encouragement with
Cardinal Fleury, nor, doubtless, with Frederick II., the son of
the '' sergeant-king,'' founder in the second instance of Prussian
militarism. The friend and vassal of this king, Voltaire, who,
although Rousseau loved him, hated our author, speaks somewhere of '' the impracticable peace of the Abbé de Saint-Pierre.''

As to Rousseau himself, Madame Dupin charged him to boil
down the *Abrégé* (p); revision by the philosopher of Geneva
clarified the confused work of the Norman, but not even that
assured success. The doctrines of the Abbé de Saint-Pierre had
but slight influence upon Bentham; they were in part the source
of Kant's inspiration, and for reasons well known Kant reaped
more glory than our author. In the nineteenth and twentieth
centuries, literary historians, economists, specialists in international law, have cited his opinions as those of a mind which
was original, but above all that of a dreamer and a builder of
castles in the air. Those who have studied· him more closely
criticise either his views on history (Goumy), or his literary form
(Sainte-Beuve), or his ingenuousness and presumption (Seroux
d'Agincourt), or his singular proposal to perpetuate the frontiers
of states as they stood (Drouet). In short, he has had more
critics than defenders.

In fact, until a period very near to our own, his very numerous
works, and particularly his *Projet*, have found no readers, either
in the original or in the collection of excerpts put together by
Alletz under the title of *Les rêves d'un homme de bien* (1775), a
title which neatly embodies the two dominant traits of his
character—his boldness and his beneficence.

(o) The humorous, if grim, comparison of the great scholar has become
famous, but it has suffered at the hands of those who have quoted it. In
d'Alembert's *Eloge de Saint-Pierre* before the Academy, the motto on a grave
becomes the sign of a Dutch merchant, and in Kant, another protagonist of
everlasting peace, the sign of an inn.

(p) See Bibliography, p. 12.

Its present validity.

Yet, in our own day, the name of the Abbé de Saint-Pierre has recovered a certain lustre under the influence of the progress of international law and of the discussions aroused on the subject of international arbitration, which, as we have seen, he very intelligently made the basis of his system. Wheaton already, among specialists in public international law, has shown himself less prejudiced against him than others. Perhaps the rest will soon recognise what I have always held, that the system of the Abbé de Saint-Pierre is more important, and even is more practicable, than has been supposed.

In fact, as the experience of our time has proved, there is no other method of avoiding war and establishing peace in international affairs than that of transferring to conflicts between States the procedure which has served in the past to appease the conflicts between groups or between individuals within the State. As the historical evolution of law shows, justice must be substituted for war. The system which shall put an end to war must therefore necessarily include as essential elements: (1) an obligatory and permanent system of international arbitration, accepted by each State, and imposed upon the recalcitrant; (2) an international arbitral tribunal; (3) an international armed force which shall secure respect for the decisions of this tribunal.

A system of this kind was conceived by one of the most learned internationalists of the nineteenth century, Pasquale Fiore, the author of *The Sanction of International Law*, and everyone gave him credit for a serious and well-considered scheme. With a little trouble it can be seen that Fiore's plan is that of the Abbé de Saint-Pierre, and yet the forerunner is treated as a rash adventurer, and almost as an impostor.

On the other hand the system is, more or less completely, the basis of the Covenant which forms the prologue to the Treaty of Versailles of June 28, 1919, and which established the League of Nations. This is not the place to argue that the Covenant would have gained greatly by attending more boldly to the lessons of the history of law, by adopting, that is to say, more fully the views of the Abbé de Saint-Pierre, who followed those lessons very closely without being a historian. We should run

the risk in so doing of compromising the success of the publications of the Grotius Society. Yet no one will refuse to concede
that between the Covenant and the system of the Abbé de Saint-
Pierre there are points in common (disarmament, open diplomacy,
respect for the frontiers established by treaty); no one will deny
that the " continuous adaptation," as M. Poincaré put it,
required to make perfect the provisions of the Covenant is
developing in the direction indicated by the dreamer of old; for,
to mention that only, on the one hand States are more and more
submitting to arbitration, and, on the other, the Locarno Agreements have introduced among nations a new organ of peace—the
permanent council of conciliation which the Covenant failed to
establish but which was forecast by the Abbé de Saint-Pierre in
his third article.

The great difference between the system of the Covenant and
that of the *Projet de paix perpétuelle*, that which made everyone
believe that General Smuts and President Wilson were creators,
when they were merely unconscious imitators, is that they
wished to establish by their League of Nations a Grand Alliance
of the peoples of the whole world, whereas the Abbé de Saint-
Pierre sought only to form a Grand Alliance of the rulers of
Europe.

Every honest man with a knowledge of history will concede
that a writer in the eighteenth century could think only of an
agreement between princes, for the people then scarcely counted.
But if the Abbé failed in his efforts, it will be allowed that the
fault was not in him but in the hour. The fault of the Abbé
was to be too much in advance of his time: the kings in the
eighteenth century did not understand their interest when he
pointed it out to them; the peoples in the twentieth century,
have acquired control of the government, will perhaps understand theirs better, and if the backward, as Kant expressed it,
honestly agree to " republicanise themselves," to have recourse,
that is to say, in case of a difference with their neighbours, not
to arms, but to a court of justice, the world will see, perhaps,
to the benefit of all, the peace of the Abbé de Saint-Pierre shine
upon it.

BIBLIOGRAPHY.

A. The standard editions of the works of the Abbé de Saint-Pierre.

The author's works are so numerous that they cannot be set out in full in this note. Only those are included which relate to that from which the excerpts are taken (a).

(i) *In the original.*

Mémoire pour rendre la paix perpétuelle en Europe. Cologne, 1712, chez J. le Pacifique, 12mo.

Projet pour rendre la paix perpétuelle en Europe. Utrecht, 1713, chez Antoine Shouten, 2 vol., 12mo.

Projet de traité pour rendre la paix perpétuelle entre les souverains chrétiens, pour maintenir toujours le commerce libre entre les nations, pour affermir beaucoup davantage les maisons souverains sur le trône. Proposé autrefois par Henri le Grand, roi de France, agréé par la reine Elisabeth, par Jacques Ier, roi d'Angleterre, son successeur et par la plupart des autres potentats d'Europe. Eclairci par M. l'abbé de Saint-Pierre. Utrecht, 1717, chez Antoine Shouten, 12mo. (Volume III. of the preceding work. In fact, printed by Deville at Lyon.)

Abrégé du Projet de Paix Perpétuelle, inventé par le roi Henri le Grand, approuvé par la reine Elisabeth, par le roi Jacques, son successeur, par les républiques et par divers autres potentats. Approprié à l'état présent des affaires générales de l'Europe, démontré infiniment avantageux pour tous les hommes nés et à naître en général et en particulier pour tous les souverains et pour les maisons souverains. Rotterdam, 1729,

---

(a) There is a complete bibliography drawn up by the Abbé's latest biographer in Joseph Drouet, *L'abbé de Saint-Pierre. L'homme et l'œuvre,* Paris, 1912, pp. 371-80.

chez Daniel Beman, 12mo. (Volume I. of the *Ouvrages de politique.*) 2nd ed., 1738.

Projet d'une paix perpétuelle et générale entre toutes les puissances de l'Europe. [n.p.] 1747, 12mo.

(ii) *In translation.*

A project for Settling an Everlasting Peace in Europe. First Proposed by Henry IV. of France, and approved of by Queen Elizabeth, and most of the then Princes of Europe, and now discussed at large, and made practicable. By the Abbot St. Pierre, of the French Academy. London: Printed for J. Watts. [1714]. Vol. I.

B. *The principal biographies.*

G. de Molinari: *L'Abbe de Saint-Pierre, membre exclu de l'Academie française. Sa vie et ses œuvres.* Paris, 1857.

E. Goumy: *Étude sur la vie et les écrits de l'abbé de Saint-Pierre.* Paris, 1859.

J. Drouet: *L'abbé de Saint-Pierre. L'homme et l'œuvre.* Paris, 1912.

C. *The most useful works for further study.*

(i). *Historical.*

J. J. Rousseau : *Extrait du projet de paix perpétuelle de M. l'abbé de Saint-Pierre.* [n.p.] 1761. [Reprinted by C. E. Vaughan: *The Political Writings of Jean Jacques Rousseau.* Cambridge, 1915. Vol. I.]

A Project for Perpetual Peace. By J. J. Rousseau, Citizen of Geneva. Translated from the French, with a Preface by the Translator. London: Printed for M. Cooper, in Pater-Noster Row, 1761. 2nd. ed., 1767.

A Lasting Peace through the Federation of Europe, and the State of War. By J. J. Rousseau. Translated by C. E. Vaughan. London, 1917.

Alletz: *Les rêves d'un homme de bien, ou les vues utiles et praticables de M. l'abbé de Saint-Pierre,* [etc.]. Paris, 1775.

G. Lanson: *Manuel bibliographique de la littérature*

française moderne. Vol. III. *Dix-huitème siècle.*
Paris, 1911.

(ii) *Critical.*

C. A. Sainte-Beuve: *Causeries du Lundi.* Vol. XV.

S. Siegler-Pascal: *Un contemporain égaré au* xviii^e
siècle. Paris, 1900.

C. Seroux d'Agincourt: *Exposé des projets de paix
perpétuelle de l'abbé de Saint-Pierre (et de
Henri IV.), de Bentham et de Kant.* Paris, 1905.

W. Borner: *Das Weltstaatsprojekt des Abbé de Saint-
Pierre. Ein Beitrag zur Geschichte der Weltfrieden-
sidee.* Berlin. 1913.

A. Blanchet: *Un pacifiste sous Louis XV.: La Société
des Nations de l'abbé de Saint-Pierre.* Macon, 1917.

(Anonymous): *Les Français à la recherche d'une
Société des Nations depuis le roi Henri IV. jusqu'aux
combattants de 1914.* Textes choisis et mis en ordre.
Paris, 1920.

ABRIDGMENT OF THE PROJECT FOR EVERLASTING PEACE.

ADVERTISEMENT TO THE READER.

I have already dealt with this matter in three volumes, the last of which appeared in 1716. I wrote then for a Public little instructed; the subject was quite new; and so it was necessary to treat it at greater length. But as for the last ten years there has been much discussion of this work at large, and in particular among the diplomats, I write now for those who are better informed about the affairs of Europe, and who wish to find in brief and within one volume those parts of the three which are of most importance. I have not failed to add several new considerations, particularly in relation to contemporary conditions, which have changed much in twenty years.

The book falls naturally into two parts. In the first I prove five most important propositions; and in the second I explain difficulties, and reply to the principal objections, while for those which are less important the Reader, if he is curious, may seek the answer to them in the larger work, for this abridgment is intended for those who have already read the other, or who, on account of their superior enlightenment, have no need to read it.

*   *   *   *   *   *   *

These are the five propositions I claim to prove.

FIRST PROPOSITION.

It is very unwise to assume that treaties, made or to be made, will always be observed, and that there will be for any length of time, neither civil wars nor foreign wars, so long as the Sovereigns of Europe shall have failed to sign five fundamental articles of general alliance.

These five articles will be found in the course of the explanation of this proposition.

SECOND PROPOSITION.

These five articles are sufficient to give perfect surety for the execution of treaties past and future, and to render secure peace both foreign and domestic.

THIRD PROPOSITION.

The most important business of the Emperor is to secure the signature of these five fundamental articles by the greatest possible number of other Sovereigns.

FOURTH PROPOSITION.

The most important business of the King of France is to secure the signature of the five fundamental articles by the greatest possible number of Sovereigns.

FIFTH PROPOSITION.

The most important business of all the other Rulers of Europe is to secure the signature of the fundamental treaty by the greatest possible number of Sovereigns.

NOTE.

For the rest, I do not claim to guarantee that the Sovereigns will follow their true interest, but only that if they follow it they will make the perpetuity and perfect solidity of peace the end of their most important negotiations. I claim to show that it is not to their true interest to remain as they are, in partnerships and alliances which are partial and temporary, with the alternatives of a peace which is really no more than a truce, or ruinous and very dangerous wars which are really perpetual, and are interrupted only by uncertain truces, and that their true interest is to escape from this pernicious situation that they may enjoy, by means of a lasting fellowship, the immense advantages which a perfectly certain peace would bring to them and to their Royal Houses.

PART I.

PROOF OF THE FIVE PROPOSITIONS.

I ask the Reader, as he does in geometry, not to pass from one proposition to another if the proofs of that which he has read do not appear to him sufficient. In this case he should re-read them, lest the failure of conviction should arise from lack of attention upon his part, and not by the fault of the Author. But if after a second reading he still has doubts, let him make a note of them that he may see whether he will not find an explanation in what follows. Those who will not give themselves this trouble will never be certain of their convictions, and consequently will never be in a position to convince others.

FIRST PROPOSITION TO BE PROVED.

It is very unwise to assume that treaties, made or to be made, will always be observed, and that there will be for any length of time no foreign wars, so long as the Sovereigns of Europe shall have failed to sign the five fundamental articles of general alliance which are absolutely necessary to render peace durable.

The treaties of Munster, the Pyrenees, Aix-la-Chapelle, Nimeguen, Ryswick, Utrecht, Baden, London, Vienna, and Hanover, and other treaties, have regulated the principal differences which existed at that time between the Sovereigns of Europe; but as those who were then the weaker thereby gave up for a time part of their claims for fear of losing much more of their territory by continuing the war, the more part of the weaker Signatories made a mental reservation to make good, at a more favourable opportunity, that is to say in a period of superior

power, the rights, the claims, which they made a show of ceding for all time in these several treaties.

*   *   *   *   *   *   *

This state of mind in the contracting Sovereigns who cede by force has always caused the wisest statesmen to regard such peace as false peace, and as a mere treaty of truce for an indefinite period. For to secure a real peace it would be necessary that the Sovereigns should have taken among themselves definite measures to prevent, by a sufficient and salutary fear, him who thought himself the stronger from resuming arms in order to realise by new victories and conquests his new or his old claims.

Now those who thought to lose by the treaty were unwilling to consent to take measures to render it perfectly durable, since they did not then consider as very profitable compensations for their claims the great advantages which they would have derived from a perfectly unalterable peace. They did not then think that they could ever arrive at a treaty which could render peace certain and perpetual, and so they did not believe the advantages which such a peace ought to secure to be actually real compensations for, and incomparably more valuable and more certain than, their claims old and new.

But as for the last nine or ten years people in Europe have begun to read the great Design of Henry the Great to render peace certain, and as it has been made evident in my larger work that it is not impossible to end without war, either by way of mediation, or by provisional and then definitive award, all the present and future differences of the Princes of Europe through their Plenipotentiaries in permanent congress, people have also begun to recognise as possible and real the great advantages, and in consequence the very desirable compensations, which would accrue to each Sovereign, in place of his claims, by means of *a certain peace, and general and perpetual alliance for the preservation to each of the allies of the territory and all the rights which they actually possess under the latest treaties.*

This opinion has led many statesmen to believe that in future negotiations the Sovereigns should not content themselves with regulating thereby their future differences, but that, to insure the execution of the articles of treaties precedent and subsequent,

for the preservation of that which they actually possess, [and] for the regulation of events which they cannot foresee, they should at last take steps among themselves to prevent any of the allies from resuming war 1º. On the one hand by depriving the more powerful, by means of leagues between a great number of the less powerful, of all hope of making any conquest; and 2º. On the other, by holding out to him who would resume arms the prospect of considerable and inevitable loss.

The wisest, therefore, have in these last few years begun to hope that there may be far more certainty in future negotiations in Europe than they have hopéd for hitherto from past negotiations. But there is really nothing to hope for so long as diplomatic conferences separate without agreeing upon such articles as may be sufficient to preserve their union, in spite of future grounds of difference, in the same way as subjects of the same state are always one body, in spite of their lawsuits.

As there are some people who cannot persuade themselves that the allies, who are at present so peaceful, would wish to break the peace in the future, it has seemed to me necessary to show that it is impossible but that war should be rekindled among them, unless they agree upon the five fundamental articles for the regulation of their future disputes without war.

Families which exist within permanent societies, and have the good fortune to have laws and Judges, armed both to regulate their claims and to secure by a salutary fear the mutual execution, whether of the laws of the State, or of their reciprocal agreements, or of the decisions of their Judges, have full security that they shall have their future claims regulated without ever being obliged to take up arms one against another, or to burn, plunder, and destroy one another. They have full security for the execution of their treaties, and that the execution of their agreements shall last as long as the state of which they are part. They have security that, in order to settle their differences, they will never be exposed to the terrible misfortune of war between family and family.

The heads of these families know that he who should take up arms and should use violence against his adversary, instead of having recourse to the Judges appointed by the authority of the State, has no hope of increasing his revenue by force and

violence, and that, on the contrary, he would be severely and inevitably punished if he used violence. So that they may have disputes and lawsuits, but the families have never to fear incomparably greater evils between them, namely, the murder, fire, and pillage caused by resort to arms, which we are spared by recourse to Judges infinitely superior in force to those who have been condemned.

Unfortunately for the Sovereign Heads of some families, they have not *yet* agreed either to form among them a *permanent society*, either for the preservation of their persons, or the preservation of their States, or to set up among themselves a permanent Tribunal, both to secure the execution of their past agreements and to regulate without war their future claims and disputes. They have, up to the present, no real security either that their treaties shall be executed, or that their differences shall be regulated by mediation or award; and, what is of the utmost importance, they have no security that their differences shall be regulated and settled without their being exposed to the fatal misfortunes of war.

The Prince who shall desire the duration of peace, and that each of the allies shall be preserved in his Estates and in all the rights of which he is in actual possession, will make no difficulty in signing the five articles necessary to procure the duration of this peace. But the Sovereign who intends shortly to take up arms in order to dispossess his neighbour will shelter himself under various pretexts from signing them, and then he will render himself suspect; [and] wise and pacific Princes will be justly alarmed, and this alarm will produce in them a still greater disposition to a strict and firm union for their mutual defence, which will have excellent results for them all. They will owe this strict union to a proper distrust of the refusal of their enemy to sign these five articles.

It is certain that there are always perpetual sources of dispute between neighbouring Sovereigns, and that, unless it shall be agreed upon by them that these shall be regulated provisionally by a plurality of the voices of the Sovereigns their Allies not party thereto, these disputes, however small may be the subject thereof, cannot be terminated, save they undergo all the misfortunes and all the hazards of war.

The signature of, or the refusal to sign, these five articles are the true touchstone to try the pacific or ambitious temper of Sovereigns.

1º. The bulk of the cessions and promises made under previous treaties have only been made, by those who yielded them in spite of themselves and for fear of losing still more by the continuation of the war than by the treaties. Thus those who yielded have only yielded in appearance and until the first occasion when they shall with impunity be able to recover what they have yielded or some equivalent. Thus, in the present situation of Europe there is no complete security for the duration of peace.

2º. There must be no mistake. Such is the temper of him who makes a surrender that there is no surrender which can prevent him from a war which he can conduct with advantage. The allies, it is true, can promise the guarantee of these cessions. But what is to prevent the Allies themselves from falling out, and from forming party alliances against one another? Does not the past teach us to divine the future? And will not, then, the promise of a guarantee become an empty promise, and the security against war a mere chimera? So that, so long as Europe will not adopt a permanent [system of] arbitration, there will be no complete security for the continuation of peace.

3º. Besides the cessions which are extorted by force, it is impossible but that there should constantly arise grounds upon which one can complain of another; it may be in the matter of boundaries, or of commerce between their Subjects, or because the treaties have left cases for which they make no provision, or wherein they are not sufficiently clear; and, therefore, without a permanent [system of] arbitration, there is no sufficient security against war, and no complete security for the duration of peace.

4º. Do not deaths [and] marriages between Sovereigns give rise from time to time to new rights and new claims to succession? And however far-seeing Sovereigns may be, they cannot make provision for all possible cases, and often they do not want to do so. And when they have made provision, what security is there for execution? Therefore the system of war gives no complete security for the duration of peace.

5º. Anyone who should take the trouble to write down the

demands made respectively, one upon the other, by two neighbouring Sovereigns, each year for four or five years, either upon
their own account or upon that of their Subjects, and consequently [still more] among a larger number of Sovereigns,
would produce a big book. Now, how many mutual demands
suffice to kindle war, particularly if one of the disputants is
hasty, bold, impatient, ambitious, unjust; if he thinks himself
superior in force, in allies; and if he only needs a pretext to
begin hostilities? Then, unless Europe changes its constitution
by some treaty, there is no complete security for the duration
of peace.

6°. Again, war cannot exist between neignbouring Sovereigns
without [other] neighbouring Princes being forced to take part
for fear of allowing the stronger to become too great and to
recover too much, when he may shortly become their enemy. So
that here is another source of war. So that, so long as the
Princes will not agree upon Judges, there is no complete security
for the duration of peace.

7°. Besides ancient claims, there are Sovereigns who still hope
for the advantages that arise from conquests. Now, how shall
he who thinks himself the stronger be willing to accept the
method of mediation or arbitration; he who fears to lose by
mediation and by arbitration, and who thinks that he can fail
in nothing of his claims by means of arms and violence; he
who is persuaded he will gain by extensive conquests far more
than his claims, under the pretext of indemnifying himself for
the cost of a just war? So that, so long as there shall be
ambitious powers, [and] so long as there shall be no powerful
Judges interested to repress their injustice, there is no security
for the duration of tranquillity and peace.

8°. Usually treaties are merely collections of mutual promises.
But we have, so far, no permanent society sufficiently powerful
and sufficiently interested in the execution of these promises.
Each of the parties can with impunity exempt himself from
the observance of them, according as he finds it to his interest
to observe them or not to observe them. So that, without a
general alliance, there is no complete security for the duration
of peace.

9°. Sovereigns do not lack pretexts to absolve themselves from

keeping their promises. Sometimes they say that, the Sovereign whom they wish to attack having begun to contravene the treaties, they consider themselves entitled to take reprisals. Sometimes there are matters of interpretation in the terms of the treaties where the interested party finds obscurity when disinterested persons see none. In short, pretexts good or bad are never wanting to the stronger that they may take advantage of their superiority. So that, in the present European system, there is no complete security for the duration of peace.

10º. Matters of complaint and mutual claims will arise between the allies, and they have no other way but war of determining them. So that any of the allies can separate himself with impunity from the alliance, in the hope that resort to arms will be very advantageous to him. And as there are Sovereigns who derive commercial profit from the declarations of war by others, and who wish to see their enemies weakened by wars, is it not probable that they will continue with all their power to rekindle them? So that, unless the signature of the five articles is begun, there is no complete security for the duration of peace.

11º. As the causes of war in the past continue to subsist without any new and sufficient preventive, it would be very unwise to think that they will not produce similar effects. The wood is dry, the fire is near, the wind blows the fire upon the wood, why should not the wood kindle? So that, so long as the Sovereigns do not sign certain new articles, there is no security for the duration of peace.

12º. Princes may receive personal injuries from their neighbours; they are, like other men, susceptible of anger and the desire for revenge. Now, who can prevent them from allying themselves with other discontented Princes to resume war? Have we not seen numbers of notable examples in every century? Another inexhaustible source of hatred and war! So that hitherto there has been no sufficient security for the duration of peace.

But if it is possible to make him who would resume war realise, in the first place, that there is a means of rendering peace in Europe certain and perpetual; in the second place, that a certain and perpetual peace would save him great expense; and, in the third place, that it would procure him advantages

greater and more real than the realisation of his claims by war, then, far from thinking of war, he will think of adopting means to render peace lasting.

These means consist in the signature of the fundamental treaty comprised in five articles.

I have had two ends in view in drawing up the articles which should compose this invaluable treaty. First, to draw them so that they shall contain everything which is absolutely necessary for the formation of an alliance, of a permanent and lasting society; and secondly, that they shall contain nothing but that which is absolutely necessary. It is for that reason that I have reduced them to so small a number, for the fewer there are the less difficult is it to correct them and to agree upon them. And these five articles, with their explanations, will give a general idea of this European Diet which will secure the peoples of Europe from war, as the Germanic Diet has actually secured the Peoples of Germany for so many centuries.

STATEMENT OF THE ARTICLES OF THE FUNDAMENTAL TREATY TO RENDER THE PEACE OF EUROPE AS LASTING AS POSSIBLE.

FIRST ARTICLE.

There shall be henceforth between the Sovereigns of Europe who shall have signed the five following articles a perpetual alliance.

1º. Mutually for all time to procure to themselves complete security from the great misfortunes of foreign war.

2º. Mutually to procure to themselves for all time complete security from the great misfortunes of civil war.

3º. Mutually to procure to themselves for all time complete security for the preservation of their States.

4º. Mutually to procure to themselves in times of weakness a much greater security for the preservation to themselves, and to their families, of the possession of sovereignty, according to the rule established in the Nation.

5º. Mutually to procure to themselves a very considerable diminution of their military expenses, while increasing their security.

6º. Mutually to procure to themselves a very considerable increase of annual profit, which will accrue from the continuity and security of commerce.

7º. Mutually to procure to themselves, with much greater ease and in much shorter time, the internal improvement or melioration of their States by the *perfecting* of the laws [and] regulations, and by the great utility of many excellent foundations.

8º. Mutually to procure to themselves complete security for the settlement of their future differences more promptly, and without risk or expense.

9º. Mutually to procure to themselves complete security for the prompt and exact execution of their treaties made or to be made.

To facilitate the formation of this alliance they agree to take for a fundamental condition *actual possession and the execution of the latest treaties*, and they are mutually bound to guarantee, one to another, that each Sovereign who shall have signed this fundamental treaty shall be preserved for all time, him and his house, in all the territory and in all the rights which he possesses at present.

They agree that the treaties, since and including the treaty of Munster, shall be executed according to their form and tenor.

And, finally, to render the grand alliance the more sure by making it the more numerous and more powerful, the grand allies agree that all Christian Sovereigns shall be invited to enter it by the signature of this fundamental treaty.

Explanation of the First Article.

1º. In this article are to be seen the nine principal effects which will certainly be produced by the general and permanent alliance, and [which are] favourable to all Christian Sovereigns. And it is these future results which are the present motives of the proposed treaty, and the certain and infinitely advantageous equivalents offered to the Sovereigns in return for their smaller,

very costly, very doubtful, and for the more part chimerical claims.

2°. Besides the motives adapted to engage the Sovereigns to form the grand alliance, there is also in these articles as the basis of the treaty the agreement to *actual possession and the execution of the latest treaties which establish rights between Sovereign and Sovereign.*

3°. It is clear that *actual possession* and the execution of the latest treaties, being established as a fixed point, effects a mutual renunciation on the part of those deprived either of actual possession or of the right which the latest treaties may give, since these claims tend to diminish in some degree the territory or the rights of which each Sovereign of the grand alliance is in *actual possession.* But this renunciation is more than compensated by the nine equivalents, that is to say, by the nine great advantages which would result both from the impossibility of war and from the perpetual duration of commerce and of peace. These advantages are explained at greater length in the course of the proof of the following propositions.

4°. There are also apparent in this first article the means to render the union certain, which is *to increase as much as possible the number of Sovereigns party to the grand alliance.* First, in order that it may be much more powerful than any one Sovereign, and even than several Sovereigns, who may wish to obstruct it in its pacific work; and, in the second place, in order that the number of Allies may be sufficient to establish a permanent [system of] arbitration or Tribunal of about twenty parties [agreed] to terminate their future differences without war.

SECOND FUNDAMENTAL ARTICLE.

Each Ally shall contribute, in proportion to the actual revenues and charges of his state, to the security and to the common expenses of the grand alliance.

This contribution shall be regulated monthly by the Plenipotentiaries of the grand allies in the place of their permanent assembly, provisionally by a plurality of voices, definitively by three-quarters of the votes.

Explanation.

1º. This second article is the second means of rendering the alliance and peace as certain as it is possible for them to be; for the daily contribution of the members, proportional and perpetual, is the fit daily and perpetual nourishment of the body politic of Europe.

2º. This contribution ought to be proportioned to the revenues of the Subjects of each Nation; and as some Nations are more heavily burdened with public debt than others, the Assessors should pay attention to that. In Germany this contribution of the Allies of the Germanic body is called a *Roman Month*. The contribution of the grand Allies of the European body would be called the *European Month*, because this contribution would be paid monthly and in advance.

THIRD FUNDAMENTAL ARTICLE.

The grand Allies have renounced, and renounce for ever, for themselves and for their successors, resort to arms in order to terminate their differences present and future, and agree henceforth always to adopt the method of conciliation by mediation of the rest of the grand Allies in the place of general assembly, or, in case this mediation should not be successful, they agree to abide by the judgment which shall be rendered by the Plenipotentiaries of the other Allies permanently assembled, provisionally by a plurality of voices, definitively by three-quarters of the votes, five years after the provisional award.

Explanation.

1º. This third article contains a third means absolutely necessary to render the grand alliance lasting. And this means is the steady preference of the salutary method, either of mediation or of arbitration, which keeps everything intact, which preserves everything, to the pernicious method of war, which oversets everything, which destroys everything.

2º. It is easy to understand that by means of the fixed and

immutable principle of *actual possession and execution of the latest treaties* future differences can never be anything but unimportant, since all possession, if it is in the least important, is always evident and effective, or determined in the latest treaties.

3°. Differences over some little frontier Villages, about some difficulty of Merchants, are of no great importance; and as the Sovereigns are all interested to regulate them justly, each will have full security that the Judges will not depart, or will only very slightly depart, from justice, even in their provisional awards. And this security ought to afford peace of mind to every reasonable person, since there is nothing important left to regulate, and that which remains will never be regulated in a way far removed from justice. The unsuccessful litigant has even the hope of a favourable award five years later, when final judgment is delivered.

4°. There will be nothing important in future to regulate between Sovereigns, except future or imminent successions to Sovereignties. But the different cases under this head will be discussed and regulated by the Allies long before the question matures: 1°. in regard to the general interest of society; 2°. in regard to the interest of the Nation; and 3°. in regard to the interest of, and justice to, the families who are claimants.

5°. The Allies then will have as the basis of their regulations the maxim *Salus populi suprema lex esto.* The preservation of the people and of the State is the supreme law; their first principle shall be the security and tranquillity of the grand alliance.

Now this security requires 1°. that the number party to the deliberations shall not be diminished; and 2°. that the territory of the five most powerful Sovereigns shall not be increased.

***

FOURTH FUNDAMENTAL ARTICLE.

If any one among the Allies refuse to execute the judgments or the regulations of the grand alliance, negotiate treaties contrary thereto, [or] make preparations for war, the grand alliance will arm, and will proceed against him until he shall execute

the said judgments or rules, or give security to make good the harm caused by his hostilities, and to repay the cost of the war according to the estimate of the Commissioners of the grand alliance.

Explanation.

1º. This fourth article contains a fourth means which is absolutely necessary to render the grand alliance indivisible, namely, a punishment, sufficient and inevitable, for him among the successors of the Allies who, without considering all the great advantages which he actually enjoys by the regulation of Europe, shall be so foolish as to seek to destroy it. For wise Princes who know their own true interests have no need of threats to keep [them] in strict union with one another, but the foolish Prince who has no clear perception of his own interest needs a wholesome fear to guide him like a child to his true interest, namely, the permanence of the association.

2º. The bonds of all associations can be reduced to two. The first, and the weakest, is hope, or the desire to advance one's well-being. The second, and the stronger, is the fear of seeing one's well-being diminished and one's misfortunes increased. Often the advantages secured by society, although very great, are overlooked for lack of attention and experience by young men, by unthinking people, and by those who are influenced by passing prejudices, so that their sympathies are not sufficiently enlisted in the preservation of society. Like children, they need the prospect of punishment, certain, near, and sufficient, awaiting anyone who shall violate the fundamental laws.

Fifth Fundamental Article.

The Allies agree that the Plenipotentiaries shall regulate finally, by a plurality of voices in their permanent assembly, all articles which may be necessary and important to procure to the grand alliance more coherence, more security, and all other possible advantages. Provided that nothing in these five fundamental articles is ever changed without the unanimous consent of all the Allies.

Explanation.

1º. It is clear that there are many more matters which it will be important to regulate, both for the security and the duration of the grand alliance, and for the common good of the Allies; but that can easily be done in the permanent assembly by Plenipotentiaries, who will have their instructions.

It will be necessary, for example, to determine who shall be the Sovereigns who shall be entitled to cast a whole vote, and who shall be the Sovereigns who shall only be entitled to a share in a vote cast by the body of those so entitled, and who shall have, each in their turn during the year, some for more and some for fewer days, according to the revenues of their States and their contributions to the common expenses, the right to act as Plenipotentiary.

It is also necessary to choose the City of peace or of assembly, at least provisionally.

It will be proper to prohibit the union of Sovereignties in one head, as it has been prohibited in the case of the Crowns of France and Spain, and to make an agreement that two Sovereignties which each cast a full vote shall never be possessed by the same Sovereign, and that succession to a Sovereignty can never be awarded, save to a Sovereign who is entitled to part of a vote only.

But there is one observation of the utmost importance which must be made, and that is that decisions, reached by a plurality provisionally and by three-quarters of the votes finally, shall never be regarded as insurmountable obstacles. This provision will remove innumerable difficulties, which the reader can imagine for himself, from the way of securing the pact.

2º. It is desirable that, in respect of the articles of the fundamental treaty, each Ally shall be sure that no change shall ever be made except with his consent, and that thus all the territory actually possessed by him shall always be preserved in its entirety to him and to his posterity by an all-powerful and immortal society.

3º. It is important, in order to facilitate the initiation of the agreement, to make the number of articles as small as possible; for the first step in every agreement is always that which is

the most difficult, and because, once this first step in an advantageous agreement has been taken, it is obviously to the interest of the parties to agree provisionally by a plurality of voices upon all that may be necessary to procure all possible advantages to the association.

Such are the five fundamental articles necessary to render peace lasting and perpetual. Now it is clear from the foregoing arguments that, so long as the Sovereigns in considerable number do not sign these or other equivalent articles, it will always be very unwise to assume that for long there will be neither civil nor foreign war in Europe. *And this is the first proposition I set out to prove.*

SECOND PROPOSITION TO BE PROVED.

THESE FIVE ARTICLES ARE SUFFICIENT TO GIVE FULL SECURITY FOR THE EXECUTION OF TREATIES, MADE OR TO BE MADE, AND TO PRODUCE A LASTING PEACE.

1º. It is clear that if several of the powers of Europe were to sign the five articles of the project of a fundamental treaty, and were jointly to solicit signature in the other Courts of Europe, they would be signed by all, or almost all, within five or six months, and it would be certain that he who refused to sign would soon give his consent for fear of being treated as a declared enemy by the general alliance.

2º. The general alliance being once formed upon the understanding that no Ally should ever take up arms against another under pain of being treated as the common enemy of the grand alliance, none of them would ever try to involve himself uselessly in heavy military expenditure against all the others.

3º. The matters of dispute between Sovereign and Sovereign will of necessity be of very little importance, such as two or three Villages more or less, and they will certainly be either settled by the mediation of the alliance or determined without war by the decision of the Allies.

4º. None of the Allies will any longer be in the position to

consider himself the stronger when he knows that he will have
all the others for his enemies. So that the flattering temptation
of great conquests will no longer tempt him to separate himself
from the grand alliance, since it will be clear to him that no
conquests are possible.

5°. Perhaps there may be a few slight disturbances within the
States of the Allies, for there are fools everywhere. But there
can never be civil war, for there is no civil war to be feared
without a leader. And who would be leaders who must be
ready to lose their goods and their lives without any hope of
success? And how could they have the least hope of success,
knowing that they must meet the forces of the whole of Europe?

6°. Those who have made certain cessions or renunciations by
treaty unwillingly, having no longer any hope of succeeding
by force, will never try to indemnify themselves by taking up
arms. So that they will happily be obliged to accept, as
equivalents and an advantageous indemnity, the great reduction
of their military expenditure, the increase of their revenue
arising from domestic and foreign commerce, and an infinity of
other great advantages which will ensue from numberless useful
regulations and foundations to further the Arts and Sciences, to
which effect can scarcely be given save during a certain and
lasting peace.

7°. Cases unforeseen or unprovided for, the import of certain
articles, quarrels between the Subjects of different Nations, may
give rise to disputes between two confederates of the body politic
of Europe, as may happen between two Citizens of the same
state. But they will be disputes of little importance at bottom
in comparison with what would have been at stake in the system
of almost perpetual war, in which the parties stand to suffer
the expense and the ruin of war, and lose their whole state.
And disputes in reality of little importance, such as those for
a Village more or less, will not cause war, for there will always
be the method of arbitration open for the determination of these
petty differences, and because resort to war will henceforth
become absolutely impossible by the establishment of an
European [system of] arbitration, formed by the signature of
the five fundamental articles.

8°. The establishment of frontier Tribunals to regulate the

differences between subjects of two Sovereigns will greatly reduce the number of mutual complaints between these Sovereigns.

9°. It is true that treaties are nothing but collections of mutual promises, and that where there is no permanent society sufficiently powerful and sufficiently interested to secure their fulfilment it is never possible to be sure that they will be fulfilled, since he who has given his word may hope to break it with impunity. But in the case of a permanent society established among the Sovereigns for the execution of treaties, and for the mutual preservation of the entire territory of which each is in *actual possession*, there is no fear that mutual promises will not be fulfilled. So that each will be in the happy position of being obliged to do justice to his neighbour, and of living for his part without fear of injustice, violence, or injury from his neighbours.

10°. So long as the Allies can secede from the alliance with impunity it cannot be regarded as a permanent society, but from this no confederate can hope to secede with impunity, or without being regarded and treated as the common enemy of all the Allies. So that not only will the great advantages of a permanent society restrain the wise and convinced Sovereigns, but the wholesome fear of punishment, adequate and inevitable, will always restrain even those Sovereigns who are exceedingly unwise and are drunk with foolish ambition.

11°. As the Allies will be authorised to provide by a plurality of votes all means proper for the security, tranquillity, and other common advantages of the general alliance, it is impossible but that, advised as they will be by the first minds in Europe, they should discover in a few years the greater part of the other measures required; and as they will be very powerful, they will easily be able to put them into execution.

It may, therefore, be concluded that the new securities which will be devised, taken with those already proposed as fundamental articles, will be sufficient to render the union indissoluble, and in consequence to render all war impossible, which is the second proposition which was to be proved.

THIRD PROPOSITION TO BE PROVED.

THE MOST IMPORTANT BUSINESS FOR THE EMPEROR IS TO SECURE THE SIGNATURE OF THE FIVE FUNDAMENTAL ARTICLES BY THE GREATEST POSSIBLE NUMBER OF SOVEREIGNS.

*   *   *   *   *   *   *

Upon the incontrovertible principle that an enterprise is the most glorious as, upon the one hand, it appears difficult, and, upon the other, is the more useful to a greater number of families within the nation and to a greater number of nations, is it not obvious that no undertaking can enter into comparison with the establishment of a system of peaceful arbitration and of an indissoluble society of Christian Sovereigns for the mutual protection in their *actual possessions* of themselves and their posterity, to assure the fulfilment of their mutual promises, to render war henceforth impossible, and to make commerce between Christian Nations perfectly secure, free, and constant?

*   *   *   *   *   *   *

Sovereign Houses have two kinds of enemies to fear, ambitious and discontented conspirators within, and ambitious and warlike Princes without. Now, if the Emperor plans new conquests, he will raise up many foreign enemies, who will have good reason to unite for their mutual defence in view of his aggrandisement; so that it may be thought improbable that he will aggrandise himself in face of the league. . . .

[But] suppose that the Emperor should make some further conquests. . . . I maintain that his conquests could not prevent his House from meeting with various periods of weakness, such as when there is a minority, or the ruler is old, or unequal to his duties. Now in these cases parties will form, and there will be civil war in his States; the conjunction of circumstances will favour attacks from within and without against his House. And it is to be remembered that, in the event of violence at home, it is of no use that the sovereign House rule over a State much more powerful than neighbouring States, since the conspirators and rebels will employ this very superiority of power

to instal themselves the sooner, and with the greater superiority of power and the more security, in spite of feeble neighbours.

What will be the principal effect of a perpetual alliance for the mutual preservation of the Allied Houses? It would be to destroy by force all attacks, or to bring to naught, by the fear that it inspires, every attempt at conspiracy, . . . since it would be conspiracy against Europe. . . .

. . . Will anyone ever be tempted to conspire against his Sovereign in order that he may put a Crown upon his head, if he sees that there are ten powerful neighbouring Sovereigns bound together for mutual defence and the protection of the poor remnants of a Royal fugitive family from conspiracy, and intimately interested to secure the punishment of the conspirator?

FOURTH PROPOSITION TO BE PROVED.

The Most Important Business of the King of France is to Secure the Signature of the Fundamental Treaty by the Greatest Possible Number of Sovereigns.

*   *   *   *   *   *   *

. . . The State which had [troops to the tune of] twelve million at its call and [to the tune of] twelve million embodied would, after signature, be infinitely more secure than it would be with [troops to the tune of] forty-eight millions without signature.

So that by signature the Sovereign, upon the one hand, increases infinitely the security of his person and that of his State, and, on the other, gains twenty-four million of revenue. . . .

It is assumed that his neighbours disarm at the same time and in the same proportion as he does, and that the Commissioners of the European confederation, by reviewing the troops of each Prince twice a year, will, for the security of all the allies, prevent all new armaments in the interior of Europe, unless by order of the general alliance.

*   *   *   *   *   *   *

FIFTH PROPOSITION TO BE PROVED.

THE MOST IMPORTANT BUSINESS OF THE OTHER SOVEREIGNS OF
    EUROPE IS TO SECURE THE SIGNATURE OF THE FIVE FUNDA-
    MENTAL ARTICLES BY THE GREATEST NUMBER OF SOVEREIGNS
    THEY CAN.

*   *   *   *   *   *   *

It is important to the King of England that seditious persons
in Parliament should not one day reduce the sovereign rights
which he enjoys. It is similarly to the interest of the English
Nation that the authority of Parliament and the present constitution of government should always be preserved in the
state in which it is now, in spite of the measures of too
tyrannical Ministers, and impatient and ill-advised Princes. Now
nothing is easier than to provide this security both for the King
and for the English Nation, since a special article can be drawn
to preserve to the King and the Nation the privileges they
possess and enjoy at present. For it is the *actual possession*
of rights of which the European confederation is guarantor, not
only between Sovereign and Sovereign, but also between certain
semi-republican peoples and their Sovereigns. Each holds to
what he *actually* possesses, and renounces his claims in
consideration of the equivalent advantages which ensue from
universal and lasting tranquillity.

PART II.

OBJECTIONS AND ANSWERS.

ADVERTISEMENT TO THE READER.

Although I have tried, as well as I was able, to make the matter so clear that I could forestall objections, I have not expected that no difficulties would be raised. There are always difficulties. This arises from two sources, which will never be exhausted. One is that the author, familiar with his own ideas, sees clearly what others without that familiarity only see darkly. He cannot put himself with sufficient exactness in the position of his readers to see where in his work there is lack of clarity in the principles or lack of connection between the principles and the consequences, although this is essential if he is to persuade those who are judges of argument.

The other source is in the reader, who, unaccustomed to argumentative works where one part depends upon another, does not pay that attention which he must in order to remember the proposition and proofs which have gone before. So that his mind fails, by defect of memory, to hold at once so great a number of ideas which mutually sustain and confirm one another, so that he cannot see how the propositions are linked together, nor in consequence feel the force of this connection, although this is essential if he is to be persuaded and convinced. Thus it is not surprising if at the first reading he cannot for himself solve the difficulties which check him.

It happens also to some readers that, for lack of familiarity with works where it is necessary to compare different parts, each of which has a theme of a different kind, they have not good enough memories to keep them all at the same time in mind. Whence it happens that they are at a loss to make an exact comparison, and that they are, so to speak, under the necessity of deciding upon the impression made by the last

arguments they can remember, without regard for those which they have forgotten.

This trouble gives rise to another; it is that the difficulty being due merely to forgetfulness, on the part of the reader, of the proofs and reasons which have been fully set out, the author finds that he must repeat many things which he has already said. But if by my replies those who have been unable to remove the difficulties for themselves are satisfied, they will not be offended by a repetition of which they stood in need, and which they did not perceive to be a repetition until they began to understand that which they had not yet understood. As to those upon whom these objections make no impression, they have only to turn over the answers without reading them.

*   *   *   *   *

SECOND OBJECTION.

I am quite aware that, as the Sovereigns will agree as a fundamental article that each confederate shall always be preserved, him and his house, in all the territory and in all the rights of which he is in actual possession, and that promises made under the last treaties shall be fulfilled, the Emperor can never have any important dispute with any of his neighbours. But by signing the treaty he loses the advantage he enjoys of deciding any dispute by superiority of force, instead of which it will only be possible to decide it by a majority of the votes of the Sovereigns, his peers. He recognises a superiority, a Tribunal, he would not have recognised; he submits to a dependence to which he has not submitted before.

Answer.

This dependence to which the Sovereign submits by virtue of a general union amounts merely to preference for dependence upon the suffrages of his allies to dependence upon the fortune of arms in future disputes, and we shall see that preference for the method of arbitration rather than the method of war greatly reduces his dependence in all other respects.

1º. If this Sovereign recognises other Sovereigns as his Judges and superiors in disputes with his neighbours, they recognise

him for their Judge and their superior in theirs; so that he only surrenders upon the one hand what he acquires upon the other. . . . So that in this respect his account is square under the system of lasting peace between Christian Nations.

2º. He can have no disputes, except they are with his neighbours or with Subjects in rebellion against his commands. Now if he choose the method of arbitration, he will be assisted against rebels by the forces of his confederates. So that by this means he will have complete security that they will always be reduced to obedience. And is not this one great fear, that is to say one great dependence, the less?

3º. Any dependence, any mistrust of the arbiters, which the Emperor may entertain, will be small in proportion as that which is deferred to their judgment is of small importance. Now we have seen that there will never be in question any but things of small importance, of which the actual possession is not clear.

So that he will suffer no dependence, however inconsiderable. Instead of being, like every Sovereign or anyone else, in a state of dependence in respect to him whom he fears or the league which he has reason to fear, it will be found that the Emperor, in choosing the method of arbitration, as he has no longer any fear, for himself or his posterity, of any league, invasion, rebellion, or conspiracy, of any reduction of authority or rights, or of any great injury, gains twenty or even a hundredfold in respect of dependence, since that which he fears under a permanent system of arbitration and lasting peace will be twenty, a hundred, times less fearful to him than that which he and his successors have to dread under the system under which we live of almost constant war, only interrupted by truces which are short and of uncertain duration.

4º. If a Sovereign fears an unjust award on the part of the grand alliance, the injustice of the award is not more to be feared than the loss of the thing itself.

5º. If he has every year one, two, or three little matters for settlement, this dependence upon the arbiters which we are discussing becomes so slight as to be almost negligible.

6º. Not only does dependence upon the Judges decrease in proportion to the small number of suits, and in proportion to

the slight and small importance of the subject of the suit, but it decreases still further in proportion as the Judges are enlightened, fair, and fully concerned to deliver judgment with scrupulous justice. Now, in a European system of arbitration, what are likely to be the subjects of litigation? They will be, perhaps, a few personal quarrels, some trifle about frontiers, or commerce. And will it not be entirely to the interest of those who are judges to give just judgments upon these matters? When they may be, both they and their children, both sinners and sinned against; when they [also] have both frontiers and commerce to control. So that it may be said that they will all be the more anxious not to do wrong to one of the parties by deviation from mercy and justice, as they may thereby do an equal or perhaps greater wrong to themselves.

7°. Are not those arbiters the least to be feared and most to be desired, by a party to a suit, to whom he is himself an arbiter in other cases?

8°. These judgments are the less to be dreaded in that they will afford precedents in similar cases. Now it often happens that he who thinks he has lost something by arbitral award will in effect have gained, in that the decision protects him from similar claims which his neighbours might have had against him and against his successors.

9°. The Sovereign who sees the instruction of the Plenipotentiaries, and who counts the votes which will go against him, can easily avoid the shame of being condemned by adopting the method of mediation or compromise, and it is an advantage to him whose claims are unjust to be able to avoid this disgrace.

10°. I shall show that the other dependencies which are avoided by virtue of this one are much more considerable. For, in short, there are only two ways of deciding things, either by a permanent system of arbitration in a reign of lasting peace, or by the uncertain chance of a system of continual war interrupted by truces.

A Sovereign who takes up arms is not sure of being quit of them by renouncing his claim if he is the claimant, or by giving up that which is demanded of him if he is on his defence. In war he risks his whole State, since if he is completely beaten and dispossessed of everything he loses all, both that which

was in issue and a thousand times more than that which was the subject of dispute.

Now if the degree of dependence is always in proportion to the importance of the matter at issue, it is clear that dependence upon the fortune of arms in a system of war is incomparably greater than that wherein the Sovereign puts himself when he submits himself to mediators, to just arbiters, since by [the system of] European arbitration he never risks more than is in issue, and that is very little; instead of which by a system of war each of the belligerents runs the risk not only of losing the thing at issue, as he does in arbitration, but also his whole fortune, even when he is only fighting for a small matter.

11º. The cost of procuring a decision by means of force under a system of war is immense, ruinous, and a dead loss to both parties when neither has prevailed over the other and they are constrained by mutual exhaustion to make peace, or rather a truce. The expenses often amount to thirty times more than the worth of the main object. While under a permanent system of arbitration no one ever takes up arms, and the judgment of the arbiters costs nothing to the parties. . . .

12º. In the present state of the affairs of Europe there is so far from being any hope for anyone who enjoys great success being repaid the costs of his conquests, that if his neighbours see that he is making considerable conquests they will at once declare themselves against him, either to prevent him from making them, or to make him restore those which he has made.

13º. If, on the one hand, under a system of continual war mingled with truces the Sovereign can always promise himself fortunate successes and the repayment of his expenses, on the other, may he not die? Is he sure that his House will never suffer a minority, or that the sovereign House over which he has enjoyed superiority will never in the centuries to come secure in its turn superiority over his during a regency. And then supposing that this neighbouring House take from his descendants what he has taken from their ancestors, is it not clear that all the expenses and ravages of war, as much upon the one part as the other, and of a war which will have lasted several centuries, will be a dead loss for both Houses?

Is not the cost of past wars for two hundred years between the

House of France and the House of Austria at this moment a dead loss to both these Houses? And at the same time calculate to what this expense and these ravages amount, and you will see that it is worth four times more than the whole Realm of France, and that if France had all the money which war has cost her during the last two hundred years she would be worth four times more than she is worth at present.

14° This Sovereign regards his claims either as most just or as unjust. If he regards them as unjust, is there anything more hateful than to wish to do to others that which he would not like them to do to him?

If he considers them to be just, where is the wisdom of preferring that the matter should be settled by the fortune of war, which is always fickle, that is to say by chance, rather than by the judgment of arbiters enlightened and rendered just by their own interests? Is there then any comparison for a wise and judicious Prince between these two kinds of dependencies?

*   *   *   *   *   *   *

16°. . . . . In short, though the dependence in which the Emperor places himself under [a system of] permanent and mutual arbitration were not in itself very slight, though the superiority which he concedes to other Sovereigns over him were not merely equal to that which he acquired over them, though this dependence to which he submits by a system of arbitration were not infinitely less than all the tiresome dependencies from which it secures him for ever, both him and his heirs, though all these things were out of the reckoning on this side, if on the other, under a system of lasting peace, he finds advantages infinitely above those which he actually experiences under a system of war, is it not clear that the dread of this dependence upon mutual arbitration ought not to deter him? Now we have shown above the great extent of his advantages.

17°. The wisest and most powerful Sovereign must fear not only for times of weakness for his posterity. Why should he not fear these periods of weakness for himself, if, on account of old age, or illness, he should become entirely unable to work? Now he preserves himself from all ill fortune by the establishment of [a system of] arbitration, permanent and mutual between peers.

He prepares defenders for himself; constant, immortal, all-powerful protectors for himself and his posterity. And the more he increases his authority, his independence, his tranquillity, the less he will have to fear.

THIRD OBJECTION.

*   *   *   *   *   *   *

. . . This fine scheme must be looked upon rather as the wish of a good citizen than as the plan of a sober statesman: *Votum non consilium.* It is a Republic of Plato, and not a practical plan. It will not suit the corrupt understandings of the age: *Non sumus in Republica Platonis, sed in faece Romuli.*

. . . Sovereigns are men, and men are not wise enough, nor sufficiently convinced, to govern themselves by their greatest interests. . . . It is prejudice, to the shame of reason, which controls reasonable beings. . . .

Answer.

*   *   *   *   *   *   *

Let us get back from general principles to plain and definite matters. What is the problem? It has just been suggested to the King of France, the King of England, the Dutch and the other pacific Sovereigns, who have acceded to the Treaty of Hanover, that they shall subscribe to the fundamental treaty in order to render the alliance lasting.

Is it not true that there is not one of them who does not fear the break-up of their alliance, and that he will be abandoned by his allies to the resentment of a powerful enemy? Now in these circumstances is it to be believed that they will refuse the only means for rendering their alliance both indissoluble and incomparably stronger? Therefore they will sign this fundamental treaty. . . .

*   *   *   *   *   *   *

There is therefore no question of those schemes, impossible in practice, which are commonly associated with the Republic of Plato. . . .

FOURTH OBJECTION.

Is it to the interest of the King of Spain to agree to have no more voice in the deliberations of the union than the King of Portugal or the King of Denmark?

Answer.

1. Why in the deliberations of the Senate in Rome, why in the deliberations of the Senators in Venice, Genoa, and other Republics ancient and modern, has a greater voice never been given to the richer, to the more powerful, than there has to the poorest Senator? It is because the poorest has as much interest, in proportion to his fortune, that the State should take the best course, as the richest can have. Now as they are both equally interested in the common good, and as they are to be taken as equal in enlightenment, is it not natural, is it not reasonable, that they should have an equal voice in things?

*   *   *   *   *   *   *

———

SEVENTH OBJECTION.

Experience teaches us that the larger an alliance is the less ardour there is for the common interests of the alliance, and the easier it is to divide the allies, and the more difficult to keep them together.

It has also been noticed that when the alliance is large, if it is necessary that all the allies should act in concert in order that their undertakings may succeed, it is more difficult to secure this, since there is always some one who tries to contribute less or to risk less. And as the ally who deserts his alliance has hitherto only had to bear feeble reproaches, and has not had to fear any punishment for the breach of treaty, he will allow the most eager and zealous to act for the good of the confederation, and will think only of seeking for pretexts and excuses for contributing nothing. And from his example another ally will play the same game another year, and the others will be disgusted in the same way. And so the bulk of plans for large confederations have vanished in smoke.

Answer.

*   *   *   *   *   *   *

It is true that men who are in association do not always see that it is to their interest to fulfil punctually the rules of the association.   But with a wholesome fear of *a sufficient and inevitable punishment* a society can always constrain them, in spite of themselves, to act in their own true interest.

*   *   *   *   *   *   *

Eleventh Objection.

The King of Spain will never be willing to sign these five funda-mental articles unless by a separate treaty, dated on the preceding day, the King of England cedes to him Gibraltar and Port Mahon, or at least promises to surrender them to him within a specified time and under the guarantee of the grand alliance.   On the other hand the King of England will never be willing to surrender them to Spain because these places are a great support to English commerce in the Mediterranean, and Spain would have to give considerable compensation to England for that.   And Spain will never be willing to give substantial compensation.

Answer.

It is clear that when almost all the Powers of Europe shall have signed the five fundamental articles, and these shall have been seen in operation throughout Europe for two or three years, the English will then have, by virtue of this signature and this general alliance, security for their commerce incomparably greater than they at present enjoy by the possession of Gibraltar and Port Mahon.

Then these two places will be, so far as commerce is concerned, entirely useless, and will also be a source of expense to them in garrisons and the upkeep of the fortifications.   Moreover these same Ports will under the fundamental Treaty always be open to their ships, as the Ports of England will always be open to Spanish ships and to the ships of all the allies.

So that the compensation which England will be able to claim from Spain will not be considered as very large by the confederates who mediate.

*   *   *   *   *   *   *

Twelfth Objection.

I foresee an obstacle which will greatly delay the signature of the five fundamental articles. It is the mutual claims which have to be settled between the Sovereigns. . . .

*   *   *   *   *   *   *

Answer.

If you admit that the Sovereigns in congress have sense enough to see that it is possible to make peace certain and lasting by the signature of the five articles, why should they not sign them, reserving to themselves the power to pass, as arbitral mediators, upon the respective claims, actual and declared in writing, of the contending Sovereigns?

Is it not the interest of every Citizen of a Town to prevent fire being put to his neighbour's house? Is it not to the interest of the sovereign Citizens of Europe to prevent the flame of war from being rekindled, lest it should spread nearer and nearer, and lay waste the whole of Europe and in consequence their own country?

Conclusion.

The Reader has seen clearly that there will never be any security for the regular fulfilment between Sovereigns of Treaties either past or future, and that there will never be any certain security against wars civil and foreign, until some shall have begun to form a lasting alliance and all the others shall have acceded to it one after the other.

The Reader has seen with the same clearness that once this Treaty were signed there would be complete security for the

regular fulfilment of treaties past and future, and complete security that peace would be lasting.

He has seen with the same clearness that the immunity from the great misfortunes caused by civil and foreign wars, and the advantages to be derived from a lasting peace and uninterrupted trade, will be compensation infinitely more substantial and of more advantage than all the mutual claims of one Power against another which are abandoned.

It is easy to conclude that the Emperor, the King of France, the King of Spain, the King of England, the King of Poland, and the other Sovereigns of Europe, have no more pressing or important business among them than the signature of the fundamental Treaty, or of the five fundamental Articles of a general alliance and a permanent [system of] arbitration, in order to render peace perfectly secure. *And this is what I proposed to prove.*

FIRST SUPPLEMENT

TO THE ABRIDGMENT OF THE PLAN FOR A LASTING PEACE.

CONTINUATION OF THE OBJECTIONS.

*　　*　　*　　*　　*　　*　　*

NINETEENTH OBJECTION.

The spirit of chicanery which has found its way into the Diets, the Imperial Chambers, and the Aulic Council, renders suits unending. Now this spirit may find its way into the Tribunal of the Sovereigns of Europe under the shelter of some ambitious Sovereign who wishes to dissolve the union of the allies by making them disgusted with the Tribunal.

Answer.

*　　*　　*　　*　　*　　*　　*

The protraction of suits is an evil, but it is an evil a hundred times less than resort to war. . . .

It will be to the interest of all the allies of Europe to diminish the abuses of chicanery. And who is to prevent them from making at any time rules in order to avoid it? Who is to prevent them from seeing, and steadily following, the common interest of their association?

TWENTIETH OBJECTION.

Great Institutions are only gradually made. The Congress of Utrecht approached nearer to your system than that of Ryswick; the Congress of Cambrai still nearer than that of Utrecht, and the Congress of Soissons nearer than that of Cambrai. Treaties of defensive Alliance are more in fashion than ever, witness the

treaties of Vienna of 1731, and consequently accessions to these treaties have become more frequent.   The Allies have begun to promise one another mutually the guarantee and security of their States.   They have begun to agree upon mutual aid in money, in Troops, in Ships.   Their interest in preserving peace makes itself felt more and more to all Sovereigns.   But there is still a long stride to take to preserve their union itself : they must agree to a permanent [system of] arbitration with a permanent Congress to regulate their present and future differences without war.

We must endure more than a hundred years yet of war in Europe, and in consequence more than two hundred years of Sovereignty, before all rulers become fully convinced that no League, no Alliance, can be lasting without a permanent [system of] arbitration, and that therefore no power can have any security for the fulfilment of any promise, nor of any treaty, unless the general Association of the Sovereigns of Europe guarantees it.

*　　*　　*　　*　　*　　*　　*

Answer.

*　　*　　*　　*　　*　　*　　*

Is there anyone of us who, if he were first Minister to a Sovereign, would not advise him, would not press him strongly, to propose these five articles for signature to his allies? . . .

. . . Now why should not the Ministers of other Nations within thirty years have made the same studies and given the same attention to the matter as we have?   Why should they not advise their King what we would advise him were we in their place?

*　　*　　*　　*　　*　　*　　*

TWENTY-SECOND OBJECTION.

I quite understand that by your method future disputes between Sovereigns will be settled as our law-suits are; it may be by compromise and agreement by aid of Plenipotentiaries deputed to mediate in the matter, who will try to make the parties to the dispute see the rights and wrongs of the matter; it may be by a

provisional award, given in the first instance by a plurality of voices, and definitively some years later by a majority of three-quarters. But from that you argue no future dispute will ever produce war between any of the associates.

Yet a case may be discovered where your conclusion will no apply.

I will suppose, for example, that there has been a dispute between a very powerful Prince, such as the King of France, and a Prince much less powerful, such as the King of Sardinia, about some Villages or some trade matter, and that, mediation having failed, the dispute has been settled, first provisionally, and then definitively by a majority of three-quarters, in favour of the less powerful Prince.

I will suppose further that of the sixteen or seventeen Sovereigns who have participated in the decision against France, four of the most powerful in Europe have been opposed to the view of the majority. Will not then these four powers joined to France give the law to the other fifteen allied powers? And who shall prevent France from taking up arms in order to end the dispute successfully, from returning, that is to say, to the old method of ending differences by war, and from preferring this disastrous and ruinous method to the new and peaceful method of a permanent [system of] arbitration.

And so cases may arise in which European arbitration will not prevent war among the associates. And so it is useless to form an association.

Answer.

* * * * * * *

[There can be] no authority, no lasting and unchangeable peace, with the unchangeable union of all parties, without the exact observation of the fundamental agreement that *each of the allies will always accord strict obedience to the decision given by a plurality provisionally, and definitively by a majority of three-quarters* . . . all the associates have agreed to preserve each of the allies in all that he actually possesses and in all that which is actually his territory. It is in this solemn act of mutual guarantee that the security of all the allies rests.

All will always be intimately concerned to maintain this article for their own security. For if their neighbour their friend is weakened, and if their neighbour their enemy, already very powerful, is strengthened, they lose much of their own security. . . .

So that the most powerful and the least powerful will have a very great and constant interest in preventing any of the associates from abandoning the method of arbitration to resort to the method of war, and from thus reducing Europe again to the disastrous confusion of foreign and civil wars.

*   *   *   *   *   *   *

First Conclusion.

It is clear that in order to achieve an indissoluble league among Sovereigns it is absolutely necessary that they should renounce the method of war in order to settle differences which can no longer be of any great importance, since they will all be preserved in their actual possessions, and the succession of Sovereigns will be regulated and limited by the grand alliance.

Second Conclusion.

It is clear that when they cannot come to an agreement through mediators, it is necessary that they should be judged by their allies, and from that it follows that it is desirable that there should be at least twelve or fifteen allies to decide, provisionally by a plurality, definitively by a majority of three-quarters.

Third Conclusion.

It is clear also that, if the losing party could excuse himself from carrying out the decision without fear of punishment sufficiently great to make him carry out the decision, he would frequently so excuse himself, and thus would stupidly destroy the alliance and fall back thoughtlessly into the frightful calamities of anarchy.

Fourth Conclusion.

It is no less clear that unless the league is indissoluble there is neither any permanent government nor any security for the fulfilment of any promise between Sovereigns, and that in consequence there is not any security for Peace, for any truce, for the continuation of trade, for the reduction of military expenditure, for the preservation of States, [nor] for the preservation of Ruling Houses upon the Throne, and therefore that there is no security either for the fulfilment of the Pragmatic Sanction of the Emperor, or for the preservation of the protestant line upon the English Throne .

     *   *   *   *   *   *   *

General Conclusion.

1°. Without the signature of the five articles establishing a European Diet [there is] no hope of a general defensive league, and partial leagues may always lead to war.

2°. Without a general league [there can be] no sufficient number of arbiters and no permanent system of arbitration.

3°. Without a permanent [system of] arbitration to settle the differences which have arisen and will arise between two Members of the league there can be no lasting alliance.

4°. Without a general and lasting league, and without a permanent [system of] arbitration, there can be no security for the fulfilment of any promise, no lasting Peace.

5°. Without a permanent and general congress there can be no facilities for agreeing upon the articles necessary to reinforce and perfect the general defensive League, no decision upon any difference, no ruling in unforeseen cases.

6°. Without a general and lasting defensive league there can be no hope of the cessation of the evils and crimes of wars civil and foreign, no hope of concord and tolerance between Christian Nations divided by Schism and Dogmas.

SECOND SUPPLEMENT.

ADVERTISEMENT TO THE READER.

I have been reproached, and with reason, because in the course of this Work I have not drawn sufficient illustration from the formation and duration of the Germanic Diet, nor from the immense advantages which the Sovereign States, both the most and the least powerful who compose it, have derived from it for the last six hundred years, so that this second Supplement is added to show that that which has already been done on a large scale can still more easily be done on a larger. The motives which ought to encourage the formation of the European Diet, and any difficulties which that formation may encounter, are the same motives and the same difficulties which prevailed at the formation of the Germanic Diet.

*   *   *   *   *   *   *

There are a few small changes in the fundamental articles of this Supplement and in the Explanations. The Reader can take the advantage of fresh attention and further examination, or can pass them by if he has found nothing *essential* at fault in the former. For by Ministers all this must be regarded as no more than a scaffolding necessary to the building which they are to build.

FUNDAMENTAL ARTICLES.

ARTICLE I.

There shall be henceforth a lasting alliance between the Sovereigns of Europe who shall have signed the following articles.

1°. *In order to form the permanent [system of] arbitration of the Republic of Europe.*

2°. *In order thus to have full security that their present and future difficulties will always be settled without war in which they*

must run the risk of losing other things than the matter in dispute, which will never be of more than small importance to them.

3°. In order to have full and lasting security for the preservation of their persons, for the preservation of their States, complete, such as they are in actual possession of, and security for the lasting preservation of their posterity on the Throne in spite of conspiracy, sedition, and revolts of their Subjects, and also full security for the preservation of their rights in the state in which they actually possess them, according to the last Treaties.

4°. In order always to have perfect security for the full and lasting fulfilment of their mutual promises, past as well as future, under the guarantee of the Republic of Europe.

5°. In order always to have perfect liberty and security for the trade of their Subjects with Foreigners.

6°. In order always to be free from the extraordinary military expense by land and sea, which they have hitherto been obliged to incur in time of war, and to secure a great reduction of their ordinary military expenditure in time of peace, and, in consequence, in order to have much better means to spend usefully upon measures important for the augmentation of their revenues and the good of their Subjects.

EXPLANATIONS.

*   *   *   *   *   *   *

ARTICLE II.

The nineteen principal Sovereigns of Europe and their Associates shall be invited to sign these five fundamental articles for the formation of a permanent European [system of] arbitration, and they shall each have one vote. . . .

These nineteen Powers shall preside in turn each week, and shall each contribute according to their revenues and to their charges to the common expenses of the European Republic, and this contribution shall be fixed in Congress provisionally, three months after signature, by a plurality of the voices of the allies, and definitively five years later by a majority of three-quarters.

Explanation.

*   *   *   *   *   *   *

The small Republics and less powerful Princes will be
associated with a Sovereign Power to form a unit entitled
to one vote, and disputes which arise on the subject of
the votes of associated Princes will be settled by arbitration. And the part which the associated members shall
have in the nomination of Plenipotentiaries will be settled by
this permanent [system of] arbitration according to the greater
or less extent of their contribution to the good and safety of the
association. The Plenipotentiary of him who contributes double
the amount contributed by another will have double the number of
days in the course of the year on which his Plenipotentiary [sic]
will have entry into congress to record his vote.

*   *   *   *   *   *   *

Article III.

*To render the alliance perfectly secure the undersigned
Sovereigns agree that each of them shall remain in possession of
the States which they actually hold, and they have renounced, and
renounce for themselves and their successors for ever, the adoption
of the disastrous method of arms against one another as a means
of settling present or future disputes or differences between themselves, and they agree always to follow henceforth the reasonable
means of conciliation and compromise at the seat of the Congress,
by the mediation of two Plenipotentiaries nominated by the
European Diet; and in case this mediation should not be successful
they agree to abide by the decision reached provisionally by a
plurality of votes, and definitively by a majority of three-quarters
five years later, by the Plenipotentiaries of the other allies,
permanently assembled at Utrecht or elsewhere.*

*   *   *   *   *   *   *

Article IV.

*If any of the allies refuse to carry out the decisions of the
grand alliance, make preparations for war, attempt to make
Treaties inconsistent with the European Association, take up arms*

to resist or attack, or in short conduct hostilities against an ally, then the grand alliance shall put him to the ban of Europe as an enemy, and shall arm and proceed against him offensively, until he has carried out the said Decisions or Rulings, and given security to repair the injury caused by war, and to repay the cost of the war, or even the cost of preparations for war on the part of each of the allies.

  *   *   *   *   *   *   *

ARTICLE V.

The plenipotentiaries of the European Association shall always have the power, by a plurality [etc.] . . . to draw up in the Diet, upon instructions from their respective Courts, the Rules which they shall judge to be requisite to procure to the Republic of Europe and to each of its Members all the advantages possible. But nothing shall ever be changed in the five fundamental articles unless with the unanimous consent of all the Confederates.

  *   *   *   *   *   *   *

SECOND REMARK.

Cannot the fifteen Powers most interested in this defensive alliance assemble in Holland, at the Hague, one after another, by their Plenipotentiaries, and unite for the signature of these five fundamental articles, and then declare that in future wars between the other four powerful Sovereigns, the Republic of Europe will take the part of him who shall accept its arbitration?

What is there in all this any more impracticable than that which has been enacted before our eyes for centuries between the Powers of Germany for their mutual protection and in order to settle their disputes without war?

THIRD REMARK.

He who, feeling himself to be superior in force, would be Judge in his own Cause, and claims that superiority in force shall alone decide what is just between him and one who is weaker, clearly wants something which is unjust. He acts contrary to the first

rule of natural justice: *Do not to another weaker than you are that which you would not that another being the stronger should do to you, the weaker.*

From that it follows that the Sovereign who is the stronger, who in a dispute with his less powerful neighbour will not submit to arbitration, is not only unjust before God, but is also hateful in the eyes of men, who have the right to judge of the justice and the injustice of his conduct, as he has the right to judge of the merits and demerits of theirs.

From that it follows that it is not true that every Sovereign has to account for what he does to God only. For he must also account to the Public, upon whom depends his reputation.

It is true that if he is more powerful than any one of his neighbours separately, and there is no permanent union among them, God alone can punish his injustice. But that does not prevent his neighbours, the Public, and even his Subjects holding him to be unjust and hateful.

Fourth Remark.

The three [sic] propositions which I have explained in this second Supplement, appear to me to go to the root of the matter quicker, and more easily, than those which I explained in the body of this work. I have added Explanations of five new Objections. In this consists the whole of this second Supplement.

FIRST DISCOURSE.

Proposition to be Explained.

So long as there shall be no treaty of mutual defence among the Sovereigns of Europe, there will be no Power sufficiently superior in force and sufficiently interested to constrain the Sovereigns by its sole authority, and by a sufficiently wholesome fear, to settle their disputes without war, either by mediation and compromise, or by means of the award of arbiters who are their peers, and there can never be expected to be secure peace between them;

there will never be anything but an uncertain truce during which they will be obliged always to be armed at great expense in order to be on their guard, and they will never have complete security for the fulfilment of their mutual promises.

Explanation.

*   *   *   *   *   *   *

As the method of war has certain great inconveniences from which the method of resort to a permanent [system of] arbitration, sufficiently powerful and sufficiently interested to secure the execution of its decisions, is free, it is desirable to make a note of what these great inconveniences are, which do not arise under the salutary method of a permanent system of arbitration, and which are necessary accompaniments of the disastrous method of resort to superiority of force in war.

THE FIRST ILL CONSEQUENCE OF THE METHOD OF WAR.

No complete security except by the annihilation of neighbours

*   *   *   *   *   *   *

SECOND . . .

Great expense to keep on one's guard.

*   *   *   *   *   *   *

THIRD . . .

No certain protection during minorities and rebellions.

*   *   *   *   *   *   *

FOURTH . . .

No security for the fulfilment of promises.

*   *   *   *   *   *   *

FIFTH . . .

The great cost of arms.

*   *   *   *   *   *   *

SIXTH . . .

Constraint to take part in the wars of neighbours.

*   *   *   *   *   *   *

SEVENTH . . .

*Loss to the nations which are at war of the revenue
derived from trade.*

*   *   *   *   *   *   *

SECOND DISCOURSE.

PROPOSITION TO BE EXPLAINED.

*The system of the balance of power between the house of
France and the house of Austria is not sufficient to secure the
Sovereigns of Europe and their subjects from the misfortunes of
foreign and civil wars, nor consequently to give complete security
for the preservation of Sovereignties and of the sovereign houses
upon the Throne.*

*   *   *   *   *   *   *

REFLECTION.

Repetitions, which are tiresome in a Work which is read for pleasure, are for the bulk of readers necessary in an argumentative Work, particularly when the matter is very new and very important.

Those who have read a proof several times in succession are in a better position to prove it to others. For in truth you do not know a thing well unless you can easily prove it.

ADVERTISEMENT TO THE READER.

I wrote at the end of 1736 certain Observations on the last Treaties of Peace, which some of my friends think very appropriate to be placed at the end of this Work.

OBSERVATIONS ON THE LAST TREATIES OF PEACE.

* * * * * * *

FOURTH PROPOSITION.

A very powerful Sovereign who refuses to sign and thus to contribute to the establishment of a European Diet, commits a crying and irreparable injustice against the nations of Europe, and in consequence is most worthy of divine punishment in the future life.

* * * * * * *

REFLECTION.

Those who think they see insurmountable difficulties amounting to the rejection of this plan can investigate whether I have explained them sufficiently in the edition in three vol----es, and

in the abridgment in one volume. For I have answered more than a hundred objections, some frivolous, some specious, which I have been carefully collecting for more than twenty years.

I give this counsel to those who are employed in this kind of public affairs, and only to those among them who expect one day to be punished if they have failed in a duty essential to their employment, if they have been in a position by their efforts to protect the nations of Europe from very great misfortunes, and have not made the effort, and to those who hope to get to Heaven by having procured, for the service of God, great benefits to their neighbour and other men by their salutary advice. For will they ever have an opportunity of procuring greater benefits for them than those which will accrue to them from a lasting peace among Christians?

And, after all, is there in life anything more important to them than their salvation? Is there anything more important to their salvation than to procure to men, for the service of God, an infinite good? Is there to that end any endeavour more important to make than to begin to search out, and to cause to be sought out, the means for fulfilling a plan so acceptable to all Sovereigns and to all their subjects? Is there any plan which it is more important to advance by their writings, by their counsel, by their discussions?

*   *   *   *   *   *   *

Printed in Great Britain by the Eastern Press, Ltd., Reading.

A PROJECT OF
PERPETUAL PEACE

A PROJECT OF

PERPETUAL PEACE

ROUSSEAU'S ESSAY

Translated by EDITH M. NUTTALL
And printed in French and English

With an Introduction by
G. LOWES DICKINSON

LONDON
RICHARD COBDEN-SANDERSON
17 THAVIES INN

First Published in 1927

Made and Printed in Great Britain by
Hazell, Watson & Viney Ld. London and Aylesbury

INTRODUCTION

IN 1756 Rousseau was at his quiet retreat, the Hermitage, some twelve miles from Paris. It was here that he set about the task of which this brief but brilliant essay is the result.

The Abbé de Saint-Pierre (1658–1743), whom Rousseau had known slightly in his youth, was a man of indefatigable benevolence and public spirit. He had unlimited faith in the reasonableness and perfectibility of human beings and in the power of reforms to make nations happy and good. Rousseau greatly admired the Abbé and was considerably influenced by his writings.

Saint-Pierre, whose youth was spent in the studious company of Fontenelle, Malebranche and Pascal, was distinguished by a universal and critical curiosity. He was a theoretical reformer, in the highest and most disinterested sense, whose brain teemed with ingenious ideas to be applied in the realm of politics or ethics like any other inventions that are used to perfect the material machinery of civilisation. To increase the comfort and happiness of mankind and

especially of his own countrymen, was the aim
of all his projects and designs, and his passion for
the improvement of society gradually anchored
itself on the principle of utility, which he expressed
in terms not less precise than those which Bentham
is generally supposed to have invented long afterwards : " the value of a book, of a regulation, of
an institution, or of any public work is proportioned to the number and grandeur of the
actual pleasures which it procures and of the
future pleasures which it is calculated to procure
for the greatest number of men."

Saint-Pierre was the first systematic Utilitarian.
Some of his proposals were that girls should be
educated, that complete freedom should be given
to the press, that a sound coinage should be introduced, that a census should be instituted, that
the burdens of taxation should be equalised, that
a system of poor relief should be established, that
useful inventions should be rewarded, that legal
procedure should be simplified and shortened,
and that a State department should be established
for the maintenance and improvement of roads
and canals. All these reforms were rejected as
visionary by contemporary rulers, but Saint-
Pierre's benevolence found expression in acts
of private charity. He once divided his meagre
fortune with a poor friend, Varignon, and to the

end of his life he rescued destitute children and had them bred up to useful trades at his own expense.

Unfortunately in his writings, the Abbé utterly failed to make his ideas attractive. "The fact," says D'Alembert, "that he had become a member of a society * whose principal object is the perfection of style did not cause him to take any more pains how he wrote." This negligence, due to a wish to save time, was misguided even from a utilitarian standpoint. Had he taken the trouble to make his style, which was clear and natural, less monotonous or more elegant, his writings would have had a larger circulation, and his projects would have gained more adherents.

Knowing that Saint-Pierre's writings, published and unpublished, were in a chaotic condition and that at best the style was too heavy and prolix to appeal to the general reader, Rousseau asked and received from his representatives permission to edit his works. He must have begun his task at least as early as January 1756; for in that month D'Argenson writes : " Rousseau is busily engaged in the analysis of the political works of Saint-Pierre."

Rousseau set to work on two of the Abbé's

* The Academy of France.

published treatises. That on Perpetual Peace, the most celebrated and important of them all, is the one that concerns us. This famous production, written in 1712 at the time of the negotiations which resulted in the Peace of Utrecht, consisted of two volumes, containing 728 pages. Unhappily, though the time seemed favourable for reviving in a new form the project by which King Henry IV, if we may believe Sully, had a hundred years earlier hoped to put an end to the discords of Europe, Saint-Pierre's efforts at the time attracted little notice. This may no doubt be explained partly by his unpopularity in court and official circles. In fact, some years later he was expelled from the Academy for denying the title of "Great" to Louis XIV.

Rousseau soon found his self-imposed task of editor too heavy and tedious. But he performed the most valuable part of his undertaking by converting with incomparable skill the *Paix Perpétuelle* and the *Polysynodie*. There were difficulties with the censorship; but in 1761 the *Paix Perpétuelle* was published at Amsterdam. Even then only the Abstract of Saint-Pierre's work appeared. The whole work with the Criticism did not come before the public till 1782, when Rousseau had been six years in his grave.

Re-dressed in Rousseau's attractive style, the little work began to find favour, and has exercised directly or indirectly an influence both on speculative thought and on practical politics. It probably led Kant to write his treatise on *Everlasting Peace* and so founded the modern literature of the Peace movement. Such phrases, for example, as " a war, which was to have been the end of war, was about to usher in eternal peace," have a wonderfully modern ring.

It is worth recording here that William Penn had anticipated the Abbé's project at a time when Europe was undergoing the miseries of an exhausting war. In order to avert strifes between governments he advocated exactly the same measure as Saint-Pierre : " a soveraign or imperial Dyet, parliament, or state of Europe ; before which soveraign assembly should be brought all differences depending between one soveraign and another, that cannot be made up by private embassies, before the session begins ; and that if any of the soveraignties that constitute these imperial states shall refuse to submit their claims or pretensions to them, or to abide and perform the judgment thereof, and seek their remedy by arms, or delay their compliance beyond the time prefixt in their resolutions, all the other soveraignties united as one strength, shall compel the

submission and performance of the sentence with damages to the suffering party, and charges to the soveraignties, that obliged their submission : to be sure Europe would quietly obtain the so much desired and needed peace to her harassed inhabitants ; no soveraignty in Europe having the power, and therefore cannot show the will to dispute the conclusion ; and consequently peace would be procured and continued in Europe."* This is very like the procedure which the League of Nations aims at putting into practice. It is very improbable that the Abbé saw Penn's work ; but that makes their agreement all the more remarkable.

The Abbé de Saint-Pierre attended the Congress at Utrecht in 1712 and at once began to prepare his adaptation of the *Grand Dessein* —that celebrated project which Henry IV according to his minister Sully had put before Elizabeth and James I, in the hopes of devising a European settlement which would curb the power of the House of Austria and, possibly at the cost of one final war, give Europe perpetual peace. Saint-Pierre, confiding in the reasonableness of human nature, had every hope that his project

---

* Penn's Essay, written in 1693, was entitled *An Essay towards the present and future peace of Europe by the Establishment of a Europeon Diet, Parliament or Estates.*

would be realised at the time ; for France, England, Spain and the German States were exhausted by a long war brought about by the ambitions of kings and princes.

But although the statesmen were disposed to peace, they were too much under the influence of Machiavelli to share the idealism of Saint-Pierre. " You have forgotten, sir," said Cardinal Fleury, " a preliminary condition on which your five articles must depend. You must begin by sending a troop of missionaries to prepare the hearts and minds of the contracting sovereigns." To the last moment of his life the Abbé maintained the practicability of his scheme, but Rousseau throughout his task of exposition felt himself hampered by the difficulty of adapting what was already half a century old to the new conditions of European politics. According to Morley " he soon found out that the Abbé de Saint-Pierre's views were impracticable in consequence of the author's fixed idea that men are guided rather by their lights than by their passions." But Leibnitz thought the project feasible and it has ever since been the goal to which thinkers have looked in their projects to abate the evils of war.

It is certain that Kant, who in 1795 published *Zum Ewigen Frieden* (*Towards Everlasting Peace*), had studied this work, though he does not mention

Saint-Pierre or Rousseau. He had, however, in earlier works made more than one admiring reference to the latter. Kant's treatise is very brief and has a more democratic groundwork than that of Saint-Pierre ; Kant was not trying to adapt a seventeenth century solution to an eighteenth or nineteenth century problem ; his work is inspired by just indignation at the wrongful Treaty of Basle, lately concluded between Prussia and France ; and his aim was to draw up a just treaty which should settle the affairs of Europe and undo the mischief of such iniquities as that of Basle. Further he was under no such illusions as those which even Rousseau discovered in Saint-Pierre. He wrote : " A state of peace among men who live side by side is not the natural state (status naturalis), which is rather to be described as a state of war : that is to say, although there is not perhaps always open hostility, yet there is a constant threatening that an outbreak may occur. Thus the state of peace must be *established*."

Accordingly he begins by laying down general international maxims, most of which have long been accepted by practical workers for peace, e.g. that no treaty of peace must contain the germ of future wars—that no independent state shall be disposed of by other states—that

standing armies shall be abolished in course of time—that national debts (for war at least) shall be forbidden—that states shall not interfere in the internal concerns of others—that (as was afterwards attempted at Hague Conferences) brutal methods of warfare shall be prohibited.

Then coming to a concrete scheme Kant, with less detail than Saint-Pierre, proposes " the Parliament of Man, the Federation of the World," which may eventually put an end to war ; but his hopes are based on an extension of democratic or republican self-government—his principle being " that a people should unite into a state according to the only valid concepts of right, the ideas of freedom and equality."

During the nineteenth century these principles slowly made headway, especially in England under the inspiration of thinkers and statesmen like Bentham, Richard Cobden and John Bright. Respect for international law grew ; arbitration gained prestige by the settlement of the Alabama claims under Mr. Gladstone and of the Venezuelan Boundary Dispute under Lord Salisbury ; and the first Hague Conference summoned by the Czar suggested some limitation of armaments while the second carried arbitration and proposals for the humanisation of war a little further forward. After the terrible world war of 1914–1918

the Covenant of the League of Nations was incorporated in the treaty of Versailles, more than two centuries after Saint-Pierre's project. It is perhaps to be regretted that President Wilson and his collaborators did not introduce a preamble setting forth the history of the subject, the experience of modern nations, the dangers of bankruptcy and ruin arising from the cost of modern armaments, the destructive inventions, mechanical and chemical, of modern science, and the opinions of great writers from Grotius onwards on the whole subject of international law.

The *Project of Perpetual Peace*, written originally by the Abbé de Saint-Pierre, and rewritten later, with abbreviations, additions and modifications, by Jean-Jacques Rousseau, has assumed a new interest since the actual creation of the League it was written to recommend.* The condition of Europe in 1712–1713, when the Abbé wrote his book, and in 1756 when Rousseau revised it, was similar in essentials to its condition in 1914 ; and to thinkers the same remedy occurred which was at last applied in 1919. The main facts were and are very simple, though they ramify into a complicated tangle of consequences. The

---

* For the history and philosophy of Arbitration and Federation those who wish to peruse the subject may be referred to the dialogues in my friend F. W. Hirst's *Arbiter in Council.*

condition to be escaped from was international anarchy ; and the description given of that, in this little book, is as good as could be found anywhere. " Every society without laws or rulers, every union formed or maintained by chance, necessarily must degenerate into quarrels and dissensions at the first clash of circumstances. The ancient union of the nations of Europe has complicated their interests and rights in a thousand ways ; they touch one another at so many points that the least movement of one is sure to give a shock to the others ; the disaster of a rupture is in proportion to the closeness of their relations and their future quarrels are almost as cruel as civil wars." The only attempts made to put an end to this condition, previous to 1919, were those of some one Power to make itself master of all the rest. The most grandiose effort of this kind was that of Napoleon, who belongs to a date later than this book. But his failure confirms the general contention that such attempts are chimerical. For this our authors give reasons ; and one passage is curiously prophetic of the actual state of Europe in the ten years preceding 1914. " Let us suppose that two or three powerful rulers make an alliance to subdue the rest. These three potentates together, who-ever they may be, will not make up the half of

Europe. Then the other half will certainly be united against them, and they will have to conquer a force stronger than themselves. . . . I may add further that if they should have formed the alliance and put it into execution, even fairly successfully, their very successes would have the effect of sowing seeds of discord among the conquering allies, because it would be impossible for the spoils to be so equally divided that each would be satisfied with his own share, and the least fortunate would soon set himself to oppose the progress of the others, who for a like reason would not be long about quarrelling among themselves." Those who have followed the recent history of Europe will find there plenty to confirm this generalisation. Nor need we attribute to our authors any peculiar gift of prophecy. Nothing is simpler in its causes and effects than the international Anarchy. Detachment and good-will have always been able to discern both, though never, until these latest times, to initiate any change.

But now, at last, we have the League of Nations, and it will not be uninteresting nor unprofitable to compare its constitution and character with the model suggested in this book. The latter, it will be observed, includes only the states of Europe. For America at that time did not count,

save as an additional cause of quarrel for the European Powers ; China interested them only as a possibility for trade ; and Japan had not yet been rudely awakened from her slumber in the enchanted forest. The only outside Power that counted for Europe was the Turkish Empire and its appendages on the Mediterranean. Our authors made no proposal for its inclusion in their League, which would therefore be bound to have a defensive force against this possible enemy. " A body so formidable as the European Republic," we are told, " would take away from foreign countries the desire to attack any of its members." But this is questionable ; and even if it were true there was no guarantee that the European league would not itself attack the foreigner.

The existing League, formed two centuries after Saint-Pierre wrote, had to take account of the changed conditions of the world. In North America was now the most powerful State in the world, and one which had participated actively in the Great War. Japan had become a great Power on the model of western States ; and the world, however politically discordant, was nevertheless bound together by a world-wide trade. Thus the League was conceived not as European, but as world-wide ; though the abstention of the

United States and of the Soviet Republic has made two gaping wounds in its body, which weaken and distract it in all its efforts.

Further, the existing League has a constitution less absolute and uncompromising than that proposed by our authors. Their federation was to be perpetual; whereas the members of our League may withdraw after notice given. Theirs ruled war out absolutely; ours permits it, should the attempts by the League at peaceable settlement fail. Theirs was to employ immediate force against a member breaking the covenant; ours hesitates to interpret its obligations in that uncompromising sense; and though the duty of economic sanctions against an offender is clear, the methods and extent thereof remain to be worked out. Our League is thus more tentative and experimental than that proposed, in this book, for Europe. Its logic is less rigorous, but it does not follow that its practice may not be more effective.

In the machinery of government, the Project described by Rousseau and the existing League show both similarities and differences. The " permanent Diet or Congress, where the differences of the contracting parties would be regulated and settled by way of arbitration or judicial decision " may remind us of the Assembly of the

League of Nations, and the newly formed International Court. But the differences are also important. Our League has an executive, the Council, which does the main part of its work, and on this the four great Powers are all-important. This is a recognition of the actual political forces at work; but, also, of the comparative impotence of reasonable and well-informed opinion where it is not backed by force. The real test of the League will come when it has to deal faithfully, according to its own constitution and principles, with one of its powerful members. Up to the present it has never dared to risk this. But the days are early, and the world is still reeling from the aftermath of the Great War. Meantime, the League has shown its practical capacity and utility in many matters of less, but still of great, importance. This tends to make it not only indispensable, but more and more capable of assuming its proper station as the general arbiter of international affairs. Its predominance, even its survival, is not yet assured; but in its ten years of life it has a record of which it need not be ashamed.

There is one other point of great importance on which we may briefly touch. The League conceived by Saint-Pierre was one, for the most part, of absolute monarchs; and that was a

principal reason for the scepticism Rousseau dis-
plays in his concluding observations. "All the
business of kings," he writes, "or of those to
whom they delegate their duties, is concerned
with two objects alone, to extend their rule
abroad or to make it more absolute at home."
But extension of rule abroad has, as history shows,
been the object of constitutional and democratic
States as much as of their predecessors ; and
so long as that object still holds the first
place no League can be anything but a camou-
flage for national ambitions. The cure, it is
usually said, will be public opinion. But the
question, as yet untested, is whether public
opinion will have a different and better bias
than Foreign Offices. That is, indeed, one
of the great problems of democracy. Foreign
affairs do not commonly interest the ordinary
man, who is absorbed in his business and his
pleasures ; or, if he take a part in public affairs,
is apt to confine himself to party affinities and
domestic issues. So long as this attitude con-
tinues he will be, in foreign affairs, the creature
of the press. But the press is the creature of
what it supposes him to want ; and it is plainly
convinced that what he wants is the crudest
patriotic emotions uninformed by knowledge.
A public so misinstructed is the predestined

victim of every adventurer. The future of the
League must thus depend on education ; a process very slow, very difficult and continually
counteracted by the press. Rousseau refers to
the phrases used by statesmen in his time to
delude the people. " The ' public good,' he
says," " ' the welfare of the people,' ' the glory
of the nations ' seem to be warnings of approaching misery." Not less so are the phrases now
so potent with our own crowds, such as " honour,"
and " my country, right or wrong." Until men
learn to say with conviction " My country only
when it is right ; and on that point it is for the
League to pronounce," the League will have a very
precarious existence. But if it fails, civilisation
is doomed. (For modern war, equipped by
modern science, is incompatible with the continuance of an industrial civilisation.) A change
has taken place in the last century which cuts us
off absolutely from all the preceding history of
mankind. We have learned how to use or misuse
nature, and we hold in our hands the powers of
life and death. But we have not yet realised
this fact ; and when children play with dynamite,
wise men fear the consequences.

Nevertheless, the League is the one great hope
of mankind, incorporating for the first time by an
international treaty a constitutional assembly for

the purpose of preventing war and consolidating peace. And from this standpoint looking back upon the work of Saint-Pierre as clarified, abbreviated and criticised by Rousseau, we may surely praise it and prize it as a noble and noteworthy landmark in the progress not merely of philosophy but of practical statesmanship towards a higher standard of civilisation. The philanthropic zeal of the Abbé, the political genius of Rousseau and the persuasive charm of his words, have not been wasted. They helped to create an institution which, rightly used, should at last bring jarring races and warring nations into the calm and prosperous haven of perpetual peace.

G. Lowes Dickinson.

TRANSLATOR'S NOTE

MANY brilliant essays have been written in glorification of war, or to commemorate the exploits of warriors; but comparatively few great masters of style have magnified the theme of international peace. And yet: "Blessed are the peacemakers; for they shall be called the children of God." In the whole of peace literature there is nothing more perfect in form or more critically suggestive than Rousseau's brilliant essay on *Paix Perpétuelle*. As no English translation is in print, it is hoped that this new version, side by side with the French original, will be welcomed, and that the younger generation, especially in schools and universities, may be incited by the study of a French classic to ideals of a civilised world of federated nations, whose controversies will be decided not by force and bloodshed, but by the decisions of judges or the awards of arbitrators.

The translation was completed before the translator was aware that the essay had been translated by the late Charles Vaughan, the leading English authority on Rousseau. The edition must have been a very small one, and the book is no longer in print. Vaughan's translation is free and vigorous, and I am indebted to it for help in the interpretation of several difficult passages. The numbers in parentheses in the text refer to the notes at the end of the volume. These have been supplied by Mr. W. A. Hirst.

LETTRE

DE JEAN-JACQUES ROUSSEAU A M. DE BASTIDE

A Montmorency, le 5 décembre 1760.

J'AUROIS voulu, monsieur, pouvoir répondre à l'honnêteté de vos sollicitations, en concourant plus utilement à votre entreprise : mais vous savez ma résolution ; et, faute de mieux, je suis réduit, pour vous complaire, à tirer de mes anciens barbouillages le morceau ci-joint, comme le moins indigne des regards du public. Il y a six ans que M. le comte de Saint-Pierre m'ayant confié les manuscrits de feu M. l'abbé son oncle, j'avois commencé d'abréger ses écrits, afin de les rendre plus commodes à lire, et que ce qu'ils ont d'utile fût plus connu. Mon dessein étoit de publier cet abrégé en deux volumes, l'un desquels eût contenu les extraits des ouvrages, et l'autre un jugement raisonné sur chaque projet : mais, après quelque essai de ce travail, je vis qu'il ne m'étoit pas propre, et que je n'y réussirois point. J'abandonnai donc ce dessein, après l'avoir seulement exécuté sur la *Paix perpétuelle* et sur la *Polysynodie*. Je vous envoie, monsieur, le premier de ces extraits, comme un sujet inaugural pour vous qui aimez la paix, et dont les écrits la respirent. Puissions-nous la voir bientôt rétablie entre les puissances ! car entre les auteurs on ne l'a jamais vue, et ce n'est pas aujourd'hui qu'on doit l'espérer. Je vous salue, monsieur, de tout mon cœur.

ROUSSEAU.

A LETTER

FROM JEAN-JACQUES ROUSSEAU TO M. DE BASTIDE (I)

At MONTMORENCY, *December 5th*, 1760.

I WISH, Sir, I could have given a favourable answer to your kind and pressing request by assisting your enterprise to more effect : but you know my mind ; and so, for want of some better means of appeasing you, I am reduced to pick out from my past scribblings the accompanying morsel, as least undeserving the notice of the public. It is six years since the Comte de Saint-Pierre (2) committed to me the manuscripts of his uncle, the late Abbé, and I thereupon began to abridge his writings, in order that they might be more conveniently read, and that their value might be better known. I had intended to publish that abstract in two volumes, one of which would have contained extracts of the originals and the other a critical estimate of each of the projects : but, after trying my hand at the task, I saw that I was unfit for it, and that I should not succeed at it. I therefore abandoned the idea, after I had applied it to *A Perpetual Peace* and *Polysynodie* (3) alone. I address the former of these extracts to you, Sir, as a dedicatory work due to you, who love peace, and whose writings breathe of it. Would that we soon might see it restored among the Powers ! Amongst authors it has never been known, and now-a-days it is too much to expect.

I am, Sir, your most humble servant,

ROUSSEAU.

B   XXV

A PROJECT OF PERPETUAL PEACE
PROJET DE PAIX PERPÉTUELLE

PAIX PERPETUELLE

COMME jamais projet plus grand, plus beau ni plus utile, n'occupa l'esprit humain, que celui d'une paix perpétuelle et universelle entre tous les peuples de l'Europe, jamais auteur ne mérita mieux l'attention du public que celui qui propose des moyens pour mettre ce projet en exécution. Il est même bien difficile qu'une pareille matière laisse un homme sensible et vertueux exempt d'un peu d'enthousiasme ; et je ne sais si l'illusion d'un cœur véritablement humain, à qui son zèle rend tout facile, n'est pas en cela préférable à cette âpre et repoussante raison qui trouve toujours dans son indifférence pour le bien public le premier obstacle à tout ce qui peut le favoriser.

Je ne doute pas que beaucoup de lecteurs ne s'arment d'avance d'incrédulité pour résister au plaisir de la persuasion, et je les plains de prendre si tristement l'entêtement pour la sagesse. Mais j'espère que quelque âme honnête partagera l'émotion délicieuse avec laquelle je prends la plume sur un sujet si intéressant pour l'humanité. Je vais voir, du moins en idée, les

2

PERPETUAL PEACE

AS no grander, finer, or more useful project
has ever occupied the human mind than
that of a perpetual and universal Peace between
all the peoples of Europe, so no author has better
deserved the attention of the public than he who
proposes means for putting this project into
execution. It is indeed difficult to believe that
such a scheme as this can leave any man of
feeling and virtue untouched by enthusiasm ; and
I incline to think that the illusions of a truly
human heart, whose zeal takes all things as
possible, are to be preferred to that sour and
repellent reason whose indifference to the public
good is always the chief obstacle to every endeavour
to promote it.

I do not doubt that many readers will forearm
themselves with incredulity, in order to resist
the pleasure of yielding to conviction, and I
pity them for so sadly mistaking obstinacy for
wisdom. But I hope that every generous soul
will share the delight with which I take up my
pen on a subject of such concern to mankind. I
see, as in a vision, men living together in unity

3

hommes s'unir et s'aimer ; je vais penser à une douce et paisible société de frères, vivant dans une concorde éternelle, tous conduits par les mêmes maximes, tous heureux du bonheur commun ; et, réalisant en moi-même un tableau si touchant, l'image d'une félicité qui n'est point, m'en fera goûter quelques instants une véritable.

Je n'ai pu refuser ces premières lignes au sentiment dont j'étois plein. Tâchons maintenant de raisonner de sang froid. Bien résolu de ne rien avancer que je ne le prouve, je crois pouvoir prier le lecteur à son tour de ne rien nier qu'il ne le réfute ; car ce ne sont pas tant les raisonneurs que je crains, que ceux qui, sans se rendre aux preuves, n'y veulent rien objecter.

Il ne faut pas avoir long-temps médité sur les moyens de perfectionner un gouvernement quelconque pour apercevoir des embarras et des obstacles, qui naissent moins de sa constitution que de ses relations externes ; de sorte que la plupart des soins qu'il faudroit consacrer à sa police, on est contraint de les donner à sa sûreté, et de songer plus à le mettre en état de résister aux autres qu'à le rendre parfait en lui-même. Si l'ordre social étoit, comme on le prétend, l'ouvrage de la raison plutôt que des passions, eût-on tardé si long-temps à voir qu'on en a

and good will. I conjure up a sweet and peaceful society of brothers, living in eternal concord, all guided by the same principles, all happy in a common happiness, and as my imagination realises a picture so touching, an image of the unattained, I enjoy a momentary taste of true happiness.

I could not help writing these opening words in response to the feelings which filled my heart. Now let us try to reason coolly. Being determined to assert nothing that I cannot prove, I have the right to ask the reader in his turn to deny nothing he cannot refute ; for it is not the logicians I fear so much, as those who, though refusing to accept my proofs, are unwilling to formulate their objections thereto.

No long reflection on the means of perfecting any government is needed to bring into view the embarrassments and hindrances which spring less from its internal constitution than from its foreign relations ; so that the greater part of that attention which ought to be given to administration must needs be devoted to defence, and more care spent to enable it to resist other powers than to perfect its own institutions. If the social order were, as is pretended, the work of reason rather than of the passions, should we have been so long in seeing that either too much

fait trop ou trop peu pour notre bonheur ; que chacun de nous étant dans l'état civil avec ses concitoyens, et dans l'état de nature avec tout le reste du monde, nous n'avons prévenu les guerres particulières que pour en allumer de générales, qui sont mille fois plus terribles ; et qu'en nous unissant à quelques hommes nous devenons réellement les ennemis du genre humain ?

S'il y a quelque moyen de lever ces dangereuses contradictions, ce ne peut être que par une forme de gouvernement confédérative, qui, unissant les peuples par des liens semblables à ceux qui unissent les individus, soumettent également les uns et les autres à l'autorité des lois. Ce gouvernement paroît d'ailleurs préférable à tout autre, en ce qu'il comprend à-la-fois les avantages des grands et des petits états, qu'il est redoutable au dehors par sa puissance, que les lois y sont en vigueur, et qu'il est le seul propre à contenir également les sujets, les chefs et les étrangers.

Quoique cette forme paroisse nouvelle à certains égards, et qu'elle n'ait en effet été bien entendue que par les modernes, les anciens ne l'ont pas ignorée. Les Grecs eurent leurs amphictyons, les Etrusques leurs lucumonies, les Latins leurs féries, les Gaules leurs cités ; et les

6

or too little has been done for our happiness ; that, as we are each of us in the civil state with our fellow-citizens, and in the state of nature with the rest of the world, we have prevented private feuds only to fan the flames of public wars which are a thousand times more terrible ; in short mankind, by gathering itself into groups, has become its own enemy ? (4)

If there is any means of getting rid of these dangerous contradictions, it can be only by a confederative form of government, which, uniting nations by bonds similar to those which unite individuals, submits them all equally to the authority of the laws. Such a government, moreover, appears to be preferable to all others in that it comprehends at one and the same time the advantage of both large and small states, that it becomes formidable abroad by reason of its power, that its laws are rigorously enforced, and that it is the only possible way of restraining equally subjects, rulers and foreigners.

Although in some respects this method may seem new (and as a matter of fact it has really been understood by the moderns only), yet the ancients were not unacquainted with it. The Greeks had their Amphictyonic Councils, the Etruscans their Lucumonies, the Latins their Feriae and the Gauls their city-leagues, whilst

derniers soupirs de la Grèce devinrent encore illustres dans la ligue achéenne. Mais nulles de ces confédérations n'approchèrent, pour la sagesse, de celle du corps germanique, de la ligue helvétique, et des états-généraux. Que si ces corps politiques sont encore en si petit nombre et si loin de la perfection dont on sent qu'ils seroient susceptibles, c'est que le mieux ne s'exécute pas comme il s'imagine, et qu'en politique ainsi qu'en morale l'étendue de nos connoissances ne prouve guère que la grandeur de nos maux.

Outre ces confédérations publiques, il s'en peut former tacitement d'autres moins apparentes et non moins réelles, par l'union des intérêts, par le rapport des maximes, par la conformité des coutumes, ou par d'autres circonstances qui laissent subsister des relations communes entre des peuples divisés. C'est ainsi que toutes les puissances de l'Europe forment entre elles une sorte de systême qui les unit par une même religion, par un même droit des gens, par les mœurs, par les lettres, par le commerce, et par une sorte d'équilibre qui est l'effet nécessaire de tout cela, et qui, sans que personne songe en effet à le conserver, ne seroit pourtant pas si facile à rompre que le pensent beaucoup de gens.

Cette société des peuples de l'Europe n'a pas

the last expiring sighs of Greece were glorified in the Achaean League. But none of these Confederations approached in wisdom that of the Germanic Body, the Swiss League and the States-General (5). And if such institutions as these are still so few in number, and so far from the perfection which we feel they might attain, it is because the best schemes never work out exactly as they were supposed, and because, in politics as in morals, the growth of our knowledge reveals only the vast extent of our woes.

In addition to these public confederations, others less apparent but none the less real, may be tacitly formed by some union of interests, by the acceptance of a common policy, by conformity of customs, or by other circumstances which create a common bond between nations otherwise separate. Thus it is that all the European Powers form among themselves a sort of system which unites them by the same religion, the same international law, by customs, literature, commerce, and by a kind of balance, a necessary consequence of all this which, without anyone's studying actually to preserve it, would nevertheless not be quite so easy to disturb as many believe.

This society of the nations of Europe has not

9

toujours existé, et les causes particulières qui l'ont fait naître servent encore à la maintenir. En effet, avant les conquêtes des Romains, tous les peuples de cette partie du monde, barbares et inconnus les uns aux autres, n'avoient rien de commun que leur qualité d'hommes, qualité qui, ravalée alors par l'esclavage, ne différoit guère dans leur esprit de celle de brute. Aussi les Grecs, raisonneurs et vains, distinguoient-ils, pour ainsi dire, deux espéces dans l'humanité ; dont l'une, savoir la leur, étoit faite pour commander ; et l'autre, qui comprenoit tout le reste du monde, uniquement pour servir. De ce principe il résultoit qu'un Gaulois ou un Ibère n'étoit rien de plus pour un Grec que n'eût été un Cafre ou un Américain ; et les barbares eux-mêmes n'avoient pas plus d'affinité entre eux que n'en avoient les Grecs avec les uns et les autres.

Mais quand ce peuple, souverain par nature, eut été soumis aux Romains ses esclaves, et qu'une partie de l'hémisphère connu eut subi le même joug, il se forma une union politique et civile entre tous les membres d'un même empire. Cette union fut beaucoup resserrée par la maxime, ou très sage ou très insensée, de communiquer aux vaincus tous les droits des vainqueurs, et sur-tout par le fameux décret de Claude, qui

always existed, and the particular causes that gave it birth serve still to maintain it. Before the Roman conquests the peoples of this part of the world, being all barbarians and unknown to one another, had nothing in common save the quality of being men, a quality which, disgraced as it was by slavery, scarcely differed in essence from the state of the brute. Accordingly the Greeks, in the pride of their philosophy, actually divided the human kind into two species, one of which (their own, to wit) was made to rule, and the other, which comprised the rest of the world, solely to serve. From this it followed that a Gaul or Iberian was of no more account to a Greek than a Kaffir or an American Indian is to us ; and the barbarous tribes themselves were as much divided from one another as they all were from the Greeks.

When, however, this people, a Sovereign race by nature, had submitted to their slaves the Romans, and half of the known hemisphere had accepted the same yoke, there came to be formed a political and civil union between all the members of a single empire. This union was drawn closer by the principle, either a very wise or a very foolish one, of bestowing on the conquered all the rights of the conquerors, and above all by the famous decree of Claudius (6) which

incorporoit tous les sujets de Rome au nombre de ses citoyens.

A la chaîne politique qui réunissoit ainsi tous les membres en un corps se joignirent les institutions civiles et les lois, qui donnèrent une nouvelle force à ces liens, en déterminant d'une manière équitable, claire et précise, du moins autant qu'on le pouvoit dans un si vaste empire, les devoirs et les droits réciproques du prince et des sujets, et ceux des citoyens entre eux. Le code de Théodose, et ensuite les livres de Justinien, furent une nouvelle chaîne de justice et de raison, substituée à propos à celle du pouvoir souverain, qui se relâchoit très sensiblement. Ce supplément retarda beaucoup la dissolution de l'empire, et lui conserva longtemps une sorte de juridiction sur les barbares mêmes qui le désoloient.

Un troisième lien, plus fort que les précédents, fut celui de la religion : et l'on ne peut nier que ce ne soit sur-tout au christianisme que l'Europe doit encore aujourd'hui l'espèce de société qui s'est perpétuée entre ses membres ; tellement que celui de ses membres qui n'a point adopté sur ce point le sentiment des autres est toujours demeuré comme étranger parmi eux. Le christianisme, si méprisé à sa naissance, servit enfin d'asile à ses détracteurs. Après l'avoir si

incorporated all the subjects of Rome into the Roman citizenship.

To the political bond which thus united all the members in one body were joined its civil institutions and laws, which gave a new strength to these ties by determining in an equitable manner, clearly and precisely, or at least as far as possible in so vast an empire, the duties and reciprocal rights of prince and subjects, and of citizen to citizen. The Theodosian code, (7) and afterwards the law-books of Justinian were a new bond of justice and reason, opportunely substituted for that of the Imperial Power, when it was being visibly relaxed. This accrual of strength considerably delayed the dissolution of the empire, and for a long time preserved to it a sort of jurisdiction over the very barbarians who were laying it waste.

A third bond, stronger than those already mentioned, was that of religion ; and undeniably it is above all to Christianity that Europe still owes to-day the kind of society which has been perpetuated among its members. So much so, that the only one of them who has not adopted the opinions of the others in this matter has always remained a stranger among them. Christianity, so despised at its birth, served in the end as a refuge for its detractors. After having

13

cruellement et si vainement persécuté, l'empire romain y trouva les ressources qu'il n'avoit plus dans ses forces ; ses missions lui valoient mieux que des victoires ; il envoyoit des évêques réparer les fautes de ses généraux, et triomphoit par ses prêtres quand ses soldats étoient battus. C'est ainsi que les Francs, les Goths, les Bourguignons, les Lombards, les Avares et mille autres, reconnurent enfin l'autorité de l'empire après l'avoir subjugué, et reçurent, du moins en apparence, avec la loi de l'évangile celle du prince qui la leur faisoit annoncer.

Tel étoit le respect qu'on portoit encore à ce grand corps expirant, que, jusqu'au dernier instant, ses destructeurs s'honoroient de ses titres : on voyoit devenir officiers de l'empire les mêmes conquérants qui l'avoient avili ; les plus grands rois accepter, briguer même, les honneurs patriciaux, la préfecture, le consulat ; et, comme un lion qui flatte l'homme qu'il pourroit dévorer, on voyoit ces vainqueurs terribles rendre hommage au trône impérial, qu'ils étoient maîtres de renverser.

Voilà comment le sacerdoce et l'empire ont formé le lien social de divers peuples qui, sans avoir aucune communauté réelle d'intérêts, de droits ou de dépendance, en avoient une de maximes et d'opinions, dont l'influence est encore

14

persecuted it so cruelly and so vainly the Roman Empire found in it resources which its own strength could no longer provide. Christian missions were of more avail than pagan victories. Rome sent out its bishops to repair the failures of its generals ; its priests triumphed when its soldiers were beaten. Thus it was that the Franks, the Goths, the Burgundians, the Lombards, the Avars, and a thousand others finally recognised the authority of the Empire after they had conquered it, and made at least a show of accepting, along with the gospel law, the law of the prince who had made it known to them.

Such was the respect that was still paid to this great dying power that up to the last moment its destroyers gloried in its titles, and one saw the same conquerors who had humbled it become officials of the Empire. The greatest kings accepted, nay even intrigued for, the Patrician honours, the office of Prefect and of Consul, and like a lion which fawns upon the man it could devour, these terrible conquerors were to be seen rendering homage to the imperial throne which they had the power to overthrow.

This is how the Church and the Empire formed a social bond for various types of peoples who, without any real community of interests or of laws or of allegiance, had one of maxims and

demeurée quand le principe a été détruit. Le simulacre antique de l'empire romain a continué de former une sorte de liaison entre les membres qui l'avoient composé ; et Rome ayant dominé d'une autre manière après la destruction de l'empire, il est resté de ce double lien * une société plus étroite entre les nations de l'Europe, où étoit le centre des deux puissances, que dans les autres parties du monde, dont les divers peuples, trop épars pour se correspondre, n'ont de plus aucun point de réunion.

Joignez à cela la situation particulière de l'Europe, plus également peuplée, plus également fertile, mieux réunie en toutes ses parties ; le mélange continuel des intérêts que les liens du sang et les affaires du commerce, des arts, des colonies, ont mis entre les souverains ; la multitude des rivières et la variété de leur cours, qui rend toutes les communications faciles ; l'humeur inconstante des habitants, qui les porte à voyager sans cesse et à se transporter fréquemment les uns chez les autres ; l'invention de

* Le respect pour l'empire romain a tellement survécu à sa puissance, que bien des jurisconsultes ont mis en question si l'empereur d'Allemagne n'étoit pas le souverain naturel du monde ; et Barthole a poussé les choses jusqu'à traiter d'hérétique quiconque osoit en douter. Les livres des canonistes sont pleins de décisions semblables sur l'autorité temporelle de l'église romaine.

opinions, whose influence still remained when its basis had been destroyed. The ancient phantom of the Roman Empire continued to form a kind of liaison between the members who had composed it ; and since Rome's dominion survived in another form after the destruction of the Empire, this double tie* left a more closely-knit society amongst the nations of Europe, where the heart of the two powers had lain, than ever existed in other parts of the world, where the different peoples, too scattered to get into communication, had besides no focus of reunion.

Add to this that Europe has special advantages over the other continents. It is more equally populated, more evenly fertile, and more compact in all its parts. The continual blending of interests, which the ties of blood and the business of commerce, of the arts and of colonisation have formed between sovereigns ; the large number of rivers the variety of whose courses make all communications easy ; the restlessness of the inhabitants ceaselessly moving about and frequently

* Respect for the Roman Empire has so fully survived its power, that many legal authorities have questioned whether the Emperor of Germany was not the natural Sovereign of the world ; and Bartholus (8) has gone so far as to treat as a heretic anyone who dared to doubt it. The canonical books are full of similar decisions on the temporal authority of the Roman church.

l'imprimerie et le goût general des lettres, qui a mis entre eux une communauté d'études et de connoissances ; enfin la multitude et la petitesse des états, qui, jointe aux besoins du luxe et à la diversité des climats, rend les uns toujours nécessaires aux autres. Toutes ces causes réunies forment de l'Europe, non seulement, comme l'Asie ou l'Afrique, une idéale collection de peuples qui n'ont de commun qu'un nom, mais une société réelle qui a sa religion, ses mœurs, ses coutumes, et même ses lois, dont aucun des peuples qui la composent ne peut s'écarter sans causer aussitôt des troubles.

A voir, d'un autre côté, les dissentions perpétuelles, les brigandages, les usurpations, les révoltes, les guerres, les meurtres, qui désolent journellement ce respectable séjour des sages, ce brillant asile des sciences et des arts ; à considérer nos beaux discours et nos procédés horribles, tant d'humanité dans les maximes et de cruauté dans les actions, une religion si douce et une si sanguinaire intolérance, une politique si sage dans les livres et si dure dans la pratique, des chefs si bienfaisants et des peuples si misérables, des gouvernements si modérés et des guerres si cruelles ; on sait a peine comment concilier ces étranges contrarietes ; et cette fraternité prétendue des peuples de l'Europe ne

travelling beyond their own frontiers; the invention of printing and general taste for letters, which has given them a common stock of studies and knowledge; and finally the large number and small size of the states, combined with the craving for luxury and the diversities of climate, make every part of Europe necessary to every other. All these causes combined, form out of Europe no mere fanciful collection of peoples with only a name in common as in Asia and Africa, but a real society which has its religion, its manners, its customs and even its laws, from which none of the people who compose it can withdraw without at once causing trouble.

To see on the other hand the perpetual dissensions, the brigandage, the usurpations, the rebellions, the wars, the murders which daily distress this venerable abode of sages, this resplendent sanctuary of science and art, and to think of our fine talk and then of our horrible actions, so much humanity in principle, so much cruelty in deed, a religion so gentle and an intolerance so bloodthirsty, a political system so wise on paper, so harsh in practice, rulers so benevolent and peoples so miserable, governments so moderate and wars so cruel, one hardly knows how to make these strange contradictions agree; and this pretended brotherhood of the nations of Europe

semble être qu'un nom de dérision pour exprimer avec ironie leur mutuelle animosité.

Cependant les choses ne font que suivre en cela leur cours naturel. Toute société sans lois ou sans chefs, toute union formée ou maintenue par le hasard, doit nécessairement dégénérer en querelle et dissention à la première circonstance qui vient à changer. L'antique union des peuples de l'Europe a compliqué leurs intérêts et leurs droits de mille manières ; ils se touchent par tant de points, que le moindre mouvement des uns ne peut manquer de choquer les autres ; leurs divisions sont d'autant plus funestes, que leurs liaisons sont plus intimes ; et leurs fréquentes querelles ont presque la cruauté des guerres civiles.

Convenons donc que l'état relatif des puissances de l'Europe est proprement un état de guerre, et que tous les traités partiels entre quelques unes de ces puissances sont plutôt des trèves passagères que de véritables paix, soit parceque ces traités n'ont point communément d'autres garants que les parties contractantes, soit parceque les droits des uns et des autres n'y sont jamais décidés radicalement, et que ces droits mal éteints, ou les prétentions qui en tiennent lieu entre des puissances qui ne reconnoissent aucun supérieur, seront infailliblement des sources de nouvelles guerres, sitôt que

seems nothing but a term of derision to express
ironically their mutual animosity.

Nevertheless in this, things only follow their
natural course ; every society without laws or
rulers, every union formed or maintained by
chance, necessarily must degenerate into quarrels
and dissensions at the first change of circumstances.
The ancient union of the nations of Europe has
complicated their interests and rights in a thousand ways ; they touch one another at so many
points that the least movement of one is sure to
give a shock to the others ; the disaster of a
rupture is in proportion to the closeness of their
relations, and their frequent quarrels are almost
as cruel as civil wars.

Let us agree, then, that in relation to one
another the European powers are properly
speaking in a state of war, and that all the partial
treaties between particular powers represent
passing truces rather than true peace, either
because these treaties have generally no other
guarantee than that of the contracting parties,
or because the rights of the two parties are never
thoroughly settled, and that these unextinguished
rights, or, it may be, the claims of the powers
who recognise no superior, will infallibly become
sources of new wars, as soon as a change of
circumstances gives new strength to the claimants.

d'autres circonstances auront donné de nouvelles forces aux prétendants.

D'ailleurs, le droit public de l'Europe n'étant point établi ou autorisé de concert, n'ayant aucuns principes généraux, et variant incessamment selon les temps et les lieux, il est plein de règles contradictoires, qui ne se peuvent concilier que par le droit du plus fort ; de sorte que la raison, sans guide assuré, se pliant toujours vers l'intérêt personnel dans les choses douteuses, la guerre seroit encore inévitable, quand même chacun voudroit être juste. Tout ce qu'on peut faire avec de bonnes intentions, c'est de décider ces sortes d'affaires par la voie des armes, ou de les assoupir par des traités passagers : mais bientôt aux occasions qui raniment les mêmes querelles il s'en joint d'autres qui les modifient ; tout s'embrouille, tout se complique ; on ne voit plus rien au fond des choses ; l'usurpation passe pour droit, la foiblesse pour injustice ; et, parmi ce désordre continuel, chacun se trouve insensiblement si fort déplacé, que si l'on pouvoit remonter au droit solide et primitif, il y auroit peu de souverains en Europe qui ne dussent rendre tout ce qu'ils ont.

Une autre semence de guerre, plus cachée et non moins réelle, c'est que les choses ne changent point de forme en changeant de nature ;

22

Moreover, as the (public law of Europe has not been established or sanctioned by concerted action, and as it has no general principles, and varies constantly according to times and circumstances, it abounds in contradictory rules which can be reconciled only by the right of the stronger; so that reason without an assured guide, in matters of doubt being always biased towards personal considerations, war would still be inevitable, even when everyone wished to be just. All one can do with the best intentions is to decide questions of this sort by an appeal to arms or to abate the controversy by temporary treaties, but soon when occasion revives these disputes, other facts enter in which modify them ; everything becomes confused and complicated ; one no longer sees to the bottom of things ; usurpation passes for law, and weakness for wrong ; and amidst this disorder everyone finds that without his knowing it the ground beneath him has shifted, insensibly indeed yet so profoundly that if one could get back to solid and original rights there would be few sovereigns in Europe who would not have to surrender everything they possess.

Another source of war, to us less visible but no less real, is that (things do not change their form in changing their nature, that states in fact hereditary remain elective in appearance, that

que des états héréditaires en effet restent électifs en apparence ; qu'il y ait des parlements ou états nationaux dans des monarchies, des chefs héréditaires dans des républiques ; qu'une puissance dépendante d'une autre conserve encore une apparence de liberté ; que tous les peuples soumis au même pouvoir ne soient pas gouvernés par les mêmes lois ; que l'ordre de succession soit différent dans les divers états d'un même souverain ; enfin que chaque gouvernement tende toujours à s'altérer sans qu'il soit possible d'empêcher ce progrès. Voilà les causes générales et particulières qui nous unissent pour nous détruire, et nous font écrire une si belle doctrine sociale avec des mains toujours teintes de sang humain.

Les causes du mal étant une fois connues, le remède, s'il existe, est suffisamment indiqué par elles. Chacun voit que toute société se forme par les intérêts communs ; que toute division naît des intérêts opposés ; que mille événements fortuits pouvant changer et modifier les uns et les autres dès qu'il y a société, il faut nécessairement une force coactive qui ordonne et concerte les mouvements de ses membres, afin de donner aux communs intérêts et aux engagements réciproques la solidité qu'ils ne sauroient avoir par eux-mêmes.

there are parliaments or national estates in monarchies and hereditary heads of republics, that a power actually dependent on another still preserves an appearance of liberty, that all the peoples ruled by the same power are not governed by the same laws, that the order of succession is different in the different states of the same sovereign, and lastly that every government always tends to change without there being any possibility of preventing this process. These, then, are the general and particular causes which unite us in order to destroy us, and make us write our fine theories of brotherly love with hands always stained with human blood.

Once the sources of the evil are recognised, they indicate their own remedy, if any such exists. Everyone sees that all societies are moulded by common interests ; that all divisions spring from opposing interests ; that a thousand accidental occurrences can change and modify both these factors, once society is called into being ; (therefore there must necessarily be some power with sanctions to regulate and organise the movements of its members, in order to give to common interests and mutual engagements that degree of solidity which they could not assume by themselves.

Ce seroit d'ailleurs une grande erreur d'espérer que cet état violent pût jamais changer par la seule force des choses et sans le secours de l'art. Le système de l'Europe a précisément le degré de solidité qui peut la maintenir dans une agitation perpétuelle, sans la renverser tout-à-fait ; et si nos maux ne peuvent augmenter, ils peuvent encore moins finir, parceque toute grande révolution est désormais impossible.

Pour donner à ceci l'évidence necessaire, commençons par jeter un coup-d'œil général sur l'état présent de l'Europe. La situation des montagnes, des mers et des fleuves qui servent de bornes aux nations qui l'habitent, semble avoir décidé du nombre et de la grandeur de ces nations ; et l'on peut dire que l'ordre politique de cette partie du monde est, à certains égards, l'ouvrage de la nature.

En effet, ne pensons pas que cet équilibre si vanté ait été établi par personne, et que personne ait rien fait à dessein de le conserver : on trouve qu'il existe ; et ceux qui ne sentent pas en eux-mêmes assez de poids pour le rompre, couvrent leurs vues particulières du prétexte de le soutenir. Mais qu'on y songe ou non, cet équilibre subsiste, et n'a besoin que de lui-même pour se conserver, sans que personne s'en mêle ; et quand il se romproit un moment d'un

26

It would be a great mistake to hope for this state of lawlessness ever to change in the natural course of things and without artificial aid. The European system possesses just enough cohesion to allow perpetual disturbances to take place without risking its complete overthrow, and, though our woes may not increase, still less can they come to an end, because any far-reaching revolution is henceforth impossible.

In proof of this, let us begin with a summary glance at the present state of Europe. The lie of the mountains, seas and rivers, which provide the boundaries of the nations who inhabit it, seems to have decided the number and size of those nations ; and we may say that the political organisation of this part of the world is, to a certain extent, the work of nature.

In short let us not imagine that this boasted balance of power has been achieved by anyone, or that anyone has done aught with intent to maintain it ; it certainly exists, and those who do not feel themselves strong enough to break it down conceal their private ends under the pretext of supporting it. But whether one is conscious of it or not, this balance exists, and can well maintain itself without outside interference. If it should be broken for a moment on one side

côté, il se rétabliroit bientôt d'un autre : de sorte que si les princes qu'on accusoit d'aspirer à la monarchie universelle y ont réellement aspiré, ils montroient en cela plus d'ambition que de génie. Car comment envisager un moment ce projet, sans en voir aussitôt le ridicule ? comment ne pas sentir qu'il n'y a point de potentat en Europe assez supérieur aux autres pour pouvoir jamais en devenir le maître ? Tous les conquérants qui ont fait des révolutions se présentoient toujours avec des forces inattendues, ou avec des troupes étrangères et différemment aguerries, à des peuples ou désarmés, ou divisés, ou sans discipline ; mais où prendroit un prince européen des forces inattendues pour accabler tous les autres, tandis que le plus puissant d'entre eux est une si petite partie du tout, et qu'ils ont de concert une si grande vigilance ? Aura-t-il plus de troupes qu'eux tous ? Il ne le peut, ou n'en sera que plus tôt ruiné ; ou ses troupes seront plus mauvaises, en raison de leur plus grand nombre. En aura-t-il de mieux aguerries ? Il en aura moins à proportion. D'ailleurs la discipline est par-tout à peu près la même, ou le deviendra dans peu. Aura-t-il plus d'argent ? Les sources en sont communes, et jamais l'argent ne fit de grandes conquêtes. Fera-t-il une invasion subite ? La famine ou des places fortes

28

it would soon re-establish itself on another ; so
that, if the princes who were accused of aspiring
to universal monarchy did really aspire to it,
they showed therein more ambition than wit.
For how can we give a moment's consideration
to this project without seeing its absurdity ?
How not feel that there is no single potentate
in Europe so much mightier than the others as
ever to be able to become their master ? All the
conquerors who have ever caused vast upheavals
have invariably appeared with unexpectedly great
forces or with foreign troops used to some dis-
tinctive discipline, as against peoples who were
defenceless, divided, or untrained to war. But
where should a European prince find these unexpected forces with which to overwhelm the
other states, as long as the most powerful of them
represents only a small fraction of the whole, and
all the rest are alert and on their guard against
him ? Will he have more troops than all the rest
together ? He cannot, or if he has he will only be
ruined the sooner by it ; or else his troops will be
of worse quality because of their greater number.
Will his men be better trained for war ? He will
then have fewer of them in proportion. Moreover, discipline is more or less on a par everywhere, or in a short time will have become so.
Will he have more money ? The sources of

l'arrêteront à chaque pas. Voudra-t-il s'agrandir
pied-à-pied ? il donne aux ennemis le moyen de
s'unir pour résister ; le temps, l'argent et les
hommes ne tarderont pas à lui manquer. Divi-
sera-t-il les autres puissances pour les vaincre
l'une par l'autre ? Les maximes de l'Europe
rendent cette politique vaine ; et le prince le
plus borné ne donneroit pas dans ce piège. Enfin,
aucun d'eux ne pouvant avoir de ressources
exclusives, la résistance est, à la longue, égale
à l'effort, et le temps rétablit bientôt les brusques
accidents de la fortune, sinon pour chaque
prince en particulier, au moins pour la constitution générale.

Veut-on maintenant supposer à plaisir l'accord
de deux ou trois potentats pour subjuguer tout
le reste ? Ces trois potentats, quels qu'ils soient,
ne feront pas ensemble la moitié de l'Europe.
Alors l'autre moitié s'unira certainement contre
eux ; ils auront donc à vaincre plus fort qu'eux-
mêmes. J'ajoute que les vues des uns sont trop
opposées à celles des autres, et qu'il règne
une trop grande jalousie entre eux, pour qu'ils
puissent même former un semblable projet.
J'ajoute encore que, quand ils l'auroient formé,
qu'ils le mettroient en exécution, et qu'il auroit
quelques succès, ces succès mêmes seroient,
pour les conquérants alliés, des semences de

money are universal, and money never yet won
great victories. Will he make a sudden invasion ?
Famine or fortresses would stop him at every
step. Will he endeavour to win inch by
inch ? He gives his enemies the means of uniting to resist him. It will, therefore, not be
long before time, money, and men fail him.
Will he divide the other powers in order to use
some to conquer the rest ? The traditions of
Europe make such a policy a vain one, and the
most stupid of princes would not fall into that
trap. Finally, as none of them can command a
monopoly of resources, the resistance in the long
run is a match for the attack, and time soon
makes good the violent accidents of fortune, if
not for each particular prince, at least for the
general balance of power.

Let us now suppose that two or three powerful
rulers make an alliance to subdue the rest. These
three potentates together, whoever they may be,
will not make up the half of Europe. Then the
other half will certainly be united against them,
and they will have to conquer a force stronger
than themselves. I may add that their aims
are too much opposed, and that too great a
jealousy exists between them ever to permit of
their forming such a project. I may add further
that if they should have formed it, and put it into

discorde ; parcequ'il ne seroit pas possible que les avantages fussent tellement partagés, que chacun se trouvât également satisfait des siens ; et que le moins heureux s'opposeroit bientôt aux progrès des autres, qui, par une semblable raison, ne tarderoient pas à se diviser eux-mêmes. Je doute que, depuis que le monde existe, on ait jamais vu trois ni même deux grandes puissances bien unies en subjuguer d'autres sans se brouiller sur les contingents ou sur les partages, et sans donner bientôt, par leur mésintelligence, de nouvelles ressources aux foibles. Ainsi, quelque supposition qu'on fasse, il n'est pas vraisemblable que ni prince, ni ligue, puisse désormais changer considérablement et à demeure l'état des choses parmi nous.

Ce n'est pas à dire que les Alpes, le Rhin, la mer, les Pyrénées, soient des obstacles insurmontables à l'ambition ; mais ces obstacles sont soutenus par d'autres qui les fortifient, ou ramènent les états aux mêmes limites, quand des efforts passagers les en ont écartés. Ce qui fait le vrai soutien du système de l'Europe, c'est bien en partie le jeu des négociations, qui presque toujours se balancent mutuellement : mais ce

execution, even fairly successfully, their very successes would have the effect of sowing seeds of discord among the conquering Allies, because it would be impossible for the spoils to be so equally divided that each would be satisfied with his own share, and the least fortunate would soon set himself to oppose the progress of the others, who, for a like reason, would not be long about quarrelling among themselves. I doubt whether since the beginning of the world there have ever been seen three, or even two great powers uniting to subdue certain others, without falling out over their respective contributions or over the division of the spoils or later, by their own misunderstandings, giving new sources of strength to their victims. Thus whatever supposition we may invent, it is improbable that either prince or league would be able in the future to make any important or permanent change in the state of our affairs.

This does not mean that the Alps, the Rhine, the sea or the Pyrenees are barriers which no ambition can surmount ; but these barriers are supported by others which strengthen them, or serve to bring states back to their original limits after passing exertions have caused a departure from them. One of the best props of the European system, as far as it goes, is the game of

33

systême a un autre appui plus solide encore,
et cet appui c'est le corps germanique, placé
presque au centre de l'Europe, lequel en tient
toutes les autres parties en respect, et sert peut-
être encore plus au maintien de ses voisins qu'à
celui de ses propres membres : corps redoutable
aux étrangers par son étendue, par le nombre
et la valeur de ses peuples ; mais utile à tous par
sa constitution, qui, lui ôtant les moyens et la
volonté de rien conquérir, en fait l'écueil des
conquérants. Malgré les défauts de cette constitution de l'empire, il est certain que, tant qu'elle
subsistera, jamais l'équilibre de l'Europe ne sera
rompu, qu'aucun potentat n'aura à craindre
d'être détrôné par un autre, et que le traité de
Westphalie sera peut-être à jamais parmi nous la
base du systême politique. Ainsi le droit public,
que les Allemands étudient avec tant de soin,
est encore plus important qu'ils ne pensent, et
n'est pas seulement le droit public germanique,
mais, à certains égards, celui de toute l'Europe.

Mais si le présent systême est inébranlable,
c'est en cela même qu'il est plus orageux ; car il y
a, entre les puissances européennes, une action et
une réaction qui, sans les déplacer tout-à-fait,
les tient dans une agitation continuelle ; et leurs
efforts sont toujours vains et toujours renaissants,

diplomacy, which almost always maintains an even balance : but this system has another and an even firmer support, namely the (block of German nations lying almost in the centre of Europe, which holds the other parts in check and serves perhaps to safeguard its neighbours still more than its own members ; a body formidable to foreigners from its size and from the numbers and valour of its people, but useful to all by its constitution which, depriving it of both the means and will to conquer, makes it a rock on which all conquest splits. In spite of its defects, it is certain that so long as the Empire preserves this constitution, the balance of power in Europe will never be broken ; no ruler need fear being dethroned by another ; and perhaps the treaty of Westphalia will always remain the basis of our political system. Thus the legal system which the Germans study with such care is even more important than they think. It is not only the common law of Germany, but in certain respects it is that of all Europe.

But if the present system is founded on a rock it is on that account all the more exposed to storms, for there flows between the European powers a tide of action and reaction which, without upsetting them altogether, keeps them in a constant state of unrest, and their efforts

comme les flots de la mer, qui sans cesse agitent sa surface sans jamais en changer le niveau ; de sorte que les peuples sont incessamment désolés sans aucun profit sensible pour les souverains.

Il me seroit aisé de déduire la même vérité des intérêts particuliers de toutes les cours de l'Europe ; car je ferois voir aisément que ces intérêts se croisent de manière à tenir toutes leurs forces mutuellement en respect : mais les idées de commerce et d'argent, ayant produit une espèce de fanatisme politique, font si promptement changer les intérêts apparents de tous les princes, qu'on ne peut établir aucune maxime stable sur leurs vrais intérêts, parceque tout dépend maintenant des systêmes économiques, la plupart fort bizarres, qui passent par la tête des ministres.* Quoi qu'il en soit, le commerce, qui tend journellement à se mettre en équilibre, ôtant à certaines puissances l'avantage exclusif

---

* Les choses ont changé depuis que j'écrivois ceci ; mais mon principe sera toujours vrai. Il est, par exemple, très aisé de prévoir que, dans vingt ans d'ici, l'Angleterre, avec toute sa gloire, sera ruinée, et, de plus, aura perdu le reste de sa liberté. Tout le monde assure que l'agriculture fleurit dans cette île ; et moi je parie qu'elle y dépérit. Londres s'agrandit tous les jours ; donc le royaume se dépeuple. Les Anglois veulent être conquérants ; donc ils ne tarderont pas d'être esclaves.

36

are always vain and always recurring, like the waves of the sea which incessantly disturb its surface without ever changing its level, so that nations are constantly afflicted without any visible advantage to their rulers.

It would be easy for me to deduce the truth of this same principle from the special interests of all the European courts; for I could easily show that these interests intermingle in such a way as makes it necessary for them to treat each other with mutual respect. But the current ideas (9) about commerce and money, having produced a kind of political fanaticism, so quickly change the superficial interests of all the princes, that it is impossible to establish any stable principle based on their real interests, because all depends now on the economic policies, for the most part fantastic, which run through the heads of ministers.* However that may be, commerce, as it tends always to a balance, takes away from

* Things have changed since 1756 (10) when I wrote this; but my principle will always be true. It is, for example, very easy to foresee that twenty years hence, England, with all her glory, will be ruined, and more than that, will have lost the remainder of her liberty. Everyone says agriculture flourishes in that island; but I dare wager it is dying out there. Every day London is growing larger; therefore the country is being depopulated. The English want to be conquerors, therefore it will not be long before they are slaves.

qu'elles en tiroient, leur ôte en même temps un des grands moyens qu'elles avoient de faire la loi aux autres.

Si j'ai insisté sur l'égale distribution de force qui résulte en Europe de la constitution actuelle, c'étoit pour en déduire une conséquence importante à l'établissement d'une association générale ; car, pour former une confédération solide et durable, il faut en mettre tous les membres dans une dépendance tellement mutuelle, qu'aucun ne soit seul en état de résister à tous les autres, et que les associations particulières qui pourroient nuire à la grande y rencontrent des obstacles suffisants pour empêcher leur exécution ; sans quoi la confédération seroit vaine, et chacun seroit réellement indépendant, sous une apparente sujétion. Or, si ces obstacles sont tels que j'ai dit ci-devant, maintenant que toutes les puissances sont dans une entière liberté de former entre elles des ligues et des traités offensifs, qu'on juge de ce qu'ils seroient quand il y auroit une grande ligue armée, toujours prête à prévenir ceux qui voudroient entreprendre de la détruire ou de lui résister. Ceci suffit pour montrer qu'une telle association ne consisteroit pas en délibérations vaines, auxquelles chacun pût résister impunément ; mais qu'il en naîtroit une

certain powers the exclusive advantages they would draw from it, and at the same time takes from them one of the best means they had of laying down the law to others

If I have insisted on the equal distribution of force which is the result in Europe of the present constitution, it was in order to deduce a conclusion of importance to the project for establishing a general league ; for, (to form a solid and durable Confederation, all its members must be placed in such a mutual state of dependence that not one of them alone may be in a position to resist all of the others, and that minor associations which would have the power to injure the general body may meet with sufficient hindrances to prevent their formation, without which the Confederation would be vain, and each would be really independent under an apparent subjection) But if these obstacles are such as I have just described, now that all the Powers are entirely free to form leagues amongst themselves and to make offensive alliances, it can be surmised what they will become when there is a great armed League always ready to prevent those who undertake to destroy or resist it. This is enough to show that such an association would not consist in useless deliberations which each could defy with impunity, but that an efficient Power would

39

puissance effective, capable de forcer les ambitieux à se tenir dans les bornes du traité général.

Il résulte de cet exposé trois vérités incontestables. L'une, qu'excepté le Turc, il règne entre tous les peuples de l'Europe une liaison sociale imparfaite, mais plus étroite que les nœuds généraux et lâches de l'humanité. La seconde, que l'imperfection de cette société rend la condition de ceux qui la composent pire que la privation de toute société entre eux. La troisième, que ces premiers liens, qui rendent cette société nuisible, la rendent en même temps facile à perfectionner ; en sorte que tous ses membres pourroient tirer leur bonheur de ce qui fait actuellement leur misère, et changer en une paix éternelle l'état de guerre qui règne entre eux.

Voyons maintenant de quelle maniere ce grand ouvrage, commencé par la fortune, peut être achevé par la raison ; et comment la société libre et volontaire qui unit tous les états européens, prenant la force et la solidité d'un vrai corps politique, peut se changer en une confédération réelle. Il est indubitable qu'un pareil établissement donnant à cette association la perfection qui lui manquoit, en détruira l'abus, en étendra les avantages, et forcera toutes les parties à

spring from it, capable of forcing ambitious nations to keep within the limits of the general treaty.

The above survey leads inevitably to three conclusions. The first is, that with the exception of the Turk, there exists among the peoples of Europe a social relation, imperfect, but closer than the loose and general bonds of humanity ; the second is, that the imperfection of this society makes the condition of those who compose it worse than if there were no society at all amongst them. The third is, that these primitive ties which render this society harmful, at the same time render it easy to perfect ; so that all its members might discover their happiness in that which at present causes their misery, and change the state of war which exists amongst them into a perpetual peace.

Let us now see in what way this great work, begun by chance, can be brought to perfection by reason, and how the free and voluntary fellowship which unites the European States, by assuming the strength and stability of a true political body, can be changed into a real Confederation. It is beyond doubt that such a settlement by giving to this association the perfection it lacks will destroy the abuse of it, increase its advantages, and force all parties to

concourir au bien commun : mais il faut pour
cela que cette confédération soit tellement
générale, que nulle puissance considérable ne s'y
refuse ; qu'elle ait un tribunal judiciaire qui
puisse établir les lois et les règlements qui doivent
obliger tous les membres ; qu'elle ait une force
coactive et coërcitive pour contraindre chaque
état de se soumettre aux délibérations communes,
soit pour agir, soit pour s'abstenir ; enfin, qu'elle
soit ferme et durable, pour empêcher que les
membres ne s'en détachent à leur volonté, sitôt
qu'ils croiront voir leur intérêt particulier contraire à l'intérêt général. Voilà les signes certains
auxquels on reconnoîtra que l'institution est
sage, utile et inébranlable. Il s'agit maintenant
d'étendre cette supposition, pour chercher
par analyse quels effets doivent en résulter,
quels moyens sont propres à l'établir, et quel
espoir raisonnable on peut avoir de la mettre en
exécution.

Il se forme de temps en temps parmi nous
des espèces de diètes générales sous le nom de
congrès, où l'on se rend solennellement de tous
les états de l'Europe pour s'en retourner de
même ; où l'on s'assemble pour ne rien dire ; où
toutes les affaires publiques se traitent en particulier ; où l'on délibère en commun si la table

co-operate for the common good. But for this it is necessary that the Confederation should be so general that no considerable Power would refuse to join it ; that it should have a judicial tribunal with power to establish laws and regulations binding on all its members ; that it should have an enforcing and coercive power to constrain each state to submit to the common counsels, whether for action or for abstention. Finally, that it should be firm and enduring, so that its members should be prevented from detaching themselves from it at will the moment they think they see their own particular interest running contrary to the general interest. These are the sure signs by which the institution will be recognised as a wise, useful, and permanent one. The next point is to extend our supposition so as to find out by analysis what effects ought to result from it, what means are best adapted to establish it, and what reasonable hope we can have of putting it into execution.

From time to time there are held amongst us, under the name of congresses, general diets whither representatives of all the states of Europe solemnly go only to return as they went ; where they assemble together to say nothing ; where all public matters are handled pettily ; where there are full debates on such questions as whether

sera ronde ou carrée, si la salle aura plus ou moins de portes, si un tel plénipotentiaire aura le visage ou le dos tourné vers la fenêtre, si tel autre fera deux pouces de chemin de plus ou de moins dans une visite, et sur mille questions de pareille importance, inutilement agitées depuis trois siècles, et très dignes assurément d'occuper les politiques du nôtre.

Il se peut faire que les membres d'une de ces assemblées soient une fois doués du sens commun ; il n'est pas même impossible qu'ils veuillent sincèrement le bien public ; et, par les raisons qui seront ci-après déduites, on peut concevoir encore qu'après avoir aplani bien des difficultés ils auront ordre de leurs souverains respectifs de signer la confédération générale que je suppose sommairement contenue dans les cinq articles suivants.

Par le premier, les souverains contractants établiront entre eux une alliance perpétuelle et irrévocable, et nommeront des plénipotentiaires pour tenir, dans un lieu déterminé, une diète ou un congrès permanent, dans lequel tous les différents des parties contractantes seront réglés et terminés par voie d'arbitrage ou de jugement.

Par le second, on spécifiera le nombre des souverains dont les plénipotentiaires auront voix

44

the table shall be round or square, whether the
hall shall have more or fewer doors, whether such
a plenipotentiary shall have his face or his back
to the window, whether another shall walk two
inches more or less in paying a call, and a thousand
other questions of equal importance, which have
been uselessly discussed for three centuries, and
which are assuredly worthy to occupy the
politicians of our own.

Possibly the members of one of the assemblies
may some day be endowed with common sense ;
it is even not impossible that they may be
sincerely interested in the public good, and for
reasons which will appear later it is even conceiv-
able that, after having smoothed away a good
many difficulties, they may receive orders from
their respective sovereigns to sign the treaty of
the general confederation, which I suppose to be
summarily contained in the five following articles.

By the first, the contracting sovereigns shall
establish amongst themselves a perpetual and
irrevocable alliance, and name plenipotentiaries
to hold in some fixed place a permanent Diet or
Congress, where the differences of contracting
parties would be regulated and settled by way of
arbitration or judicial decisions.

By the second shall be specified the number of
sovereigns whose plenipotentiaries are to have a

à la diète ; ceux qui seront invités d'accéder au
traité ; l'ordre, le temps et la manière dont la
présidence passera de l'un à l'autre par intervalles
égaux ; enfin la quotité relative des contributions,
et la manière de les lever pour fournir aux
dépenses communes.

Par le troisième, la confédération garantira a
chacun de ses membres la possession et le
gouvernement de tous les états qu'il possède
actuellement, de même que la succession élective
ou héréditaire, selon que le tout est établi par
les lois fondamentales de chaque pays ; et, pour
supprimer tout d'un coup la source des démêlés
qui renaissent incessamment, on conviendra de
prendre la possession actuelle et les derniers
traités pour base de tous les droits mutuels des
puissances contractantes ; renonçant pour jamais
et réciproquement à toute autre prétention
antérieure ; sauf les successions futures conten-
tieuses, et autres droits à échoir, qui seront tous
réglés à l'arbitrage de la diète, sans qu'il soit
permis de s'en faire raison par voies de fait, ni
de prendre jamais les armes l'un contre l'autre,
sous quelque prétexte que ce puisse être.

Par le quatrième, on spécifiera les cas où tout
allié infracteur du traité seroit mis au ban de
l'Europe, et proscrit comme ennemi public :

voice in the assembly, those who are to be invited
to agree to the treaty, the order, the time, and the
manner in which the presidency shall pass from
one to the other for equal terms, and finally the
relative quota of the contributions to the common
expenses and the manner of raising them.

By the third, the Confederation shall guarantee
to its members the possession and government of
all the states each of them controls at the moment,
as well as the succession, elective or hereditary,
according to whichever is established by the
fundamental laws of each country ; and in order
to put an end once and for all to all the disputes
which are constantly reviving, it shall be agreed
to take present possession and the latest treaties
as the basis of the mutual rights of the contracting
Powers, at the same time renouncing for ever and
reciprocally all anterior pretensions, with the
exception of future contested successions and
other rights which may fall due, and which shall
all be decided by the ruling of the Diet, no
member being permitted under any pretext
whatsoever to take the law into his own hands,
or take up arms against his fellow members.

By the fourth the cases shall be specified in
which any Ally guilty of infringing the Treaty
is to be put under the ban of Europe and pro-
claimed a common enemy—that is to say, if he

E   47

savoir, s'il refusoit d'exécuter les jugements de
la grande alliance, qu'il fît des préparatifs de
guerre, qu'il négociât des traités contraires à la
confédération, qu'il prît les armes pour lui
résister ou pour attaquer quelqu'un des alliés.

Il sera encore convenu par le même article
qu'on armera et agira offensivement, conjoin-
tement, et à frais communs, contre tout état
au ban de l'Europe, jusqu'à ce qu'il ait mis bas
les armes, exécuté les jugements et règlements de
la diète, réparé les torts, remboursé les frais, et
fait raison même des préparatifs de guerre
contraires au traité.

Enfin, par le cinquieme, les plénipotentiaires
du corps europeen auront toujours le pouvoir
de former dans la diète, à la pluralité des voix
pour la provision, et aux trois quarts des voix
cinq ans après pour la définitive, sur les instructions de leurs cours, les règlements qu'ils juge-
ront importants pour procurer à la république
européenne et à chacun de ses membres tous
les avantages possibles ; mais on ne pourra
jamais rien changer à ces cinq articles fondamen-
taux que du consentement unanime des confédérés.

Ces cinq articles, ainsi abrégés et couchés en
règles générales, sont, je ne l'ignore pas, sujets

refuse to carry out the decisions of the great Alliance, if he make preparations for war, if he negotiate treaties contrary to the terms of the Confederation, and if he take up arms to resist it or to attack any one of the Allies.

It shall be agreed also by the same article that the States shall arm and act together offensively and conjointly, and at the common expense against any state under the ban of Europe, until it shall have laid down its arms, carried out the sentences and rulings of the Congress, repaired the wrongs, refunded the costs, and even given compensation for any warlike preparations it may have made contrary to the Treaty.

Lastly, by the fifth article, the plenipotentiaries of the European Federal Body shall always have the power, on the instructions of their Courts, to frame in the Diet by a majority of votes, provisionally (and by a three-quarter majority five years afterwards, finally), the regulations which they shall judge to be important in order to secure all possible advantages to the European Republic and each one of its members ; but it shall never be possible to change any of these five fundamental articles except with the unanimous consent of all the members of the Confederation.

These five articles thus abridged and couched in general rules are, I am aware, subject to a

49

a mille petites difficultés, dont plusieurs demanderoient de longs éclaircissements : mais les petites difficultés se lèvent aisément au besoin ; et ce n'est pas d'elles qu'il s'agit dans une entreprise de l'importance de celle-ci. Quand il sera question du détail de la police du congrès, on trouvera mille obstacles et dix mille moyens de les lever. Ici il est question d'examiner, par la nature des choses, si l'entreprise est possible ou non. On se perdroit dans des volumes de riens, s'il falloit tout prévoir et répondre à tout. En se tenant aux principes incontestables, on ne doit pas vouloir contenter tous les esprits, ni résoudre toutes les objections, ni dire comment tout se fera ; il suffit de montrer que tout se peut faire.

Que faut-il donc examiner pour bien juger de ce système ? Deux questions seulement ; car c'est une insulte que je ne veux pas faire au lecteur, de lui prouver qu'en général l'état de paix est préférable à l'état de guerre.

La première question est, si la confédération proposée iroit sûrement a son but et seroit suffisante pour donner à l'Europe une paix solide et perpétuelle.

La seconde, s'il est de l'intérêt des souverains d'établir cette confédération et d'acheter une paix constante à ce prix.

thousand small difficulties, of which several would need long explanations ; but small difficulties can be removed easily at need, and they do not matter very much in such an important enterprise as this. When it becomes a question of the details of the policy of the Congress, a thousand obstacles will be found, and ten thousand means of overcoming them. Here it is a question of examining whether in the nature of things the enterprise is possible or not. We should be lost in an ocean of trivial details if we had to foresee and answer them all. Whilst keeping to unquestionable principles we must not try to please all minds, nor solve all objections, nor say how everything will be done ; it is enough to show it can be done.

What are the questions that must be put to enable us to form a correct judgment upon this system ? Two only ; for it is an insult I will not offer the reader to prove to him that in general a state of peace is to be preferred to a state of war.

The first question is whether the proposed Confederation would attain its end with certainty and be sufficient to give to Europe a solid and enduring peace ; the second, whether it is to the interest of the rulers to establish this Confederation and to purchase a stable peace at this price.

Quand l'utilité générale et particulière sera ainsi démontrée, on ne voit plus, dans la raison des choses, quelle cause pourroit empêcher l'effet d'un établissement qui ne dépend que de la volonté des intéressés.

Pour discuter d'abord le premier article, appliquons ici ce que j'ai dit ci-devant du système général de l'Europe, et de l'effort commun qui circonscrit chaque puissance à peu près dans ses bornes, et ne lui permet pas d'en écraser entierement d'autres. Pour rendre sur ce point mes raisonnements plus sensibles, je joins ici la liste des dix-neuf puissances qu'on suppose composer la république européenne ; en sorte que, chacune ayant voix égale, il y auroit dix-neuf voix dans la diète ; savoir : l'empereur des Romains, l'empereur de Russie, le roi de France, le roi d'Espagne, le roi d'Angleterre, les états-généraux, le roi de Danemarck, la Suède, la Pologne, le roi de Portugal, le souverain de Rome, le roi de Prusse, l'électeur de Bavière et ses co-associés ; l'électeur palatin et ses co-associés, les Suisses et leurs co-associés, les électeurs ecclésiastiques et leurs associés, la république de Venise et ses co-associés, le roi de Naples, le roi de Sardaigne.

Plusieurs souverains moins considérables, tels que la république de Gênes, les ducs de Modène et de Parme, et d'autres, étant omis dans cette

When its general and particular utility has been thus demonstrated, one no longer sees in the nature of things what cause could prevent the successful working of an institution which only depends on the will of those interested.

In order to discuss the first article let us apply what I have said of the general system of Europe and of the common action which limits each Power very nearly to its own frontiers and does not permit it entirely to crush others out of existence. To make my meaning clearer on this point I subjoin here a list of the nineteen Powers which may be said to compose the European Republic, so that were each one to have an equal voice there would be nineteen votes at the Congress: the Emperor of the Romans, the Emperor of Russia, the King of France, the King of Spain, the King of England, the States-General, the King of Denmark, the King of Sweden, the King of Poland, the King of Portugal, the Papal States, the King of Prussia, the Elector of Bavaria and his associates, the Elector Palatine and his associates, the Swiss Republic and its associates, the Ecclesiastical Electors with their associates, the Venetian Republic, the King of Naples, the King of Sardinia.

Several less important sovereigns, such as the Republic of Genoa, the dukes of Modena and

liste, seront joints aux moins puissants, par forme d'association, et auront avec eux un droit de suffrage, semblable au *votum curiatum* des comtes de l'empire. Il est inutile de rendre ici cette énumération plus précise, parceque, jusqu'à l'exécution du projet, il peut survenir d'un moment à l'autre des accidents sur lesquels il la faudroit réformer, mais qui ne changeroient rien au fond du système.

Il ne faut que jeter les yeux sur cette liste pour voir avec la dernière évidence qu'il n'est pas possible ni qu'aucune des puissances qui la composent soit en état de résister à toutes les autres unies en corps, ni qu'il s'y forme aucune ligue partielle capable de faire tête à la grande confédération.

Car comment se feroit cette ligue ? seroit-ce entre les plus puissants ? Nous avons montré qu'elle ne sauroit être durable ; et il est bien aisé maintenant de voir encore qu'elle est incompatible avec le système particulier de chaque grande puissance, et avec les intérêts inséparables de sa constitution. Seroit-ce entre un grand état et plusieurs petits ? mais les autres grands états, unis à la confédération, auront bientôt écrasé la ligue : et l'on doit sentir que la grande alliance étant toujours unie et armée, il lui sera facile,

Parma, and others omitted in this list would be joined to the less powerful in the form of an association, and would hold in common with them a right of suffrage similar to the *votum curiatum* of the counts of the Empire. It is useless to give a more precise enumeration here, because, until the project is carried out, events may at any moment happen which would necessitate remaking the list, but would change none of the ground-work of the system.

We have only to glance at this list to be convinced that it is not possible for any of the Powers which compose it to be in a position to oppose all the others united together in one body, nor for any partial league to be formed capable of holding its own against the great Confederation.

For how would this League be made ? Would it be drawn up between the most powerful ? We have shown that it could never last, and it is easy now to see also that it is incompatible with the special policy of each great Power, and with the interests inseparable from its Constitution. Would it then be between one great State and several little ones ? But the other great States, united to the Confederation, would soon crush the league, and obviously the great Alliance being always united and armed would find it easy by virtue of the fourth article to forestall and

55

en vertu du quatrieme article, de prévenir et d'étouffer d'abord toute alliance partielle et séditieuse qui tendroit à troubler la paix et l'ordre public. Qu'on voie ce qui se passe dans le corps germanique, malgré les abus de sa police et l'extrême inégalité de ses membres : y en a-t-il un seul, même parmi les plus puissants, qui osât s'exposer au ban de l'empire en blessant ouvertement sa constitution, à moins qu'il ne crût avoir de bonnes raisons de ne point craindre que l'empire voulût agir contre lui tout de bon?

Ainsi je tiens pour démontré que la diète européenne une fois établie n'aura jamais de rébellion à craindre, et que, bien qu'il s'y puisse introduire quelques abus, ils ne peuvent jamais aller jusqu'à éluder l'objet de l'institution. Reste à voir si cet objet sera bien rempli par l'institution même.

Pour cela, considérons les motifs qui mettent aux princes les armes à la main. Ces motifs sont, ou de faire des conquêtes, ou de se défendre d'un conquérant, ou d'affoiblir un trop puissant voisin, ou de soutenir ses droits attaqués, ou de vider un différent qu'on n'a pu terminer à l'amiable, ou enfin de remplir les engagements d'un traité. Il n'y a ni cause ni prétexte de guerre

suppress from the outset every separate and seditious Alliance which should tend to disturb the general peace and order. Let us see what happens in the German States, in spite of the abuses in their organisation and the extreme inequality of their members. Is there a single one even among the strongest of them who would dare to incur the ban of the empire by openly offending against its constitution, at least unless he had good reasons for believing that there was no fear that the empire would take strong action against him ?

Thus I maintain it to be demonstrated that the European Diet once established need fear no revolt, and that although some abuses might creep in they could never go so far as to defeat the object of the institution. It remains to be seen whether that object would be fulfilled satisfactorily by our Federal institution.

As to that, let us consider the motives which make princes take up arms. These motives are either to make conquests or to defend themselves against an invader, or to weaken a too powerful neighbour, or to maintain their own rights when assailed, or to end a quarrel which has not been settled amicably, or lastly to fulfil the engagements of a treaty. There is neither cause of nor pretext for war that you cannot place under one

57

qu'on ne puisse ranger sous quelqu'un de ces six chefs : or il est évident qu'aucun des six ne peut exister dans ce nouvel état de choses.

Premièrement, il faut renoncer aux conquêtes, par l'impossibilité d'en faire, attendu qu'on est sûr d'être arrêté dans son chemin par de plus grandes forces que celles qu'on peut avoir ; de sorte qu'en risquant de tout perdre on est dans l'impuissance de rien gagner. Un prince ambitieux, qui veut s'agrandir en Europe, fait deux choses : il commence par se fortifier de bonnes alliances, puis il tâche de prendre son ennemi au dépourvu. Mais les alliances particulières ne serviroient de rien contre une alliance plus forte, et toujours subsistante ; et nul prince n'ayant plus aucun prétexte d'armer, il ne sauroit le faire sans être aperçu, prévenu et puni par la confédération toujours armée.

La même raison qui ôte à chaque prince tout espoir de conquêtes lui ôte en même temps toute crainte d'être attaqué ; et, non seulement ses états, garantis par toute l'Europe, lui sont aussi assurés qu'aux citoyens leurs possessions dans un pays bien policé, mais plus que s'il étoit leur unique et propre défenseur, dans le même rapport que l'Europe entière est plus forte que lui seul.

of these six heads. But it is evident that none of these six motives can exist in the new state of things that I contemplate.

First, conquests will have to be renounced from the impossibility of making them, considering that everyone is sure to be stopped on the way by greater forces than those he is able to marshal; thus, whilst risking the loss of everything, it is beyond his power to gain anything. An ambitious prince who wishes to increase his possessions in Europe does two things: he begins by strengthening himself with good alliances, then he tries to take his enemy unawares. But private alliances would be of no use against the stronger alliance already in existence; and as no prince will any longer have any pretext for arming, he cannot do so without its being noticed, prevented, and punished by an ever armed Confederation.

The same reason which deprives each prince of any hope of conquests deprives him at the same time of any fear of being attacked; and not only are his estates (guaranteed to him by all Europe) assured to him just as are the private possessions of the citizens in a civilised country, but they are even more so than were he their own sole defender, in proportion as the whole of Europe is stronger than he is alone.

On n'a plus de raison de vouloir affoiblir un voisin dont on n'a plus rien à craindre ; et l'on n'en est pas même tenté, quand on n'a nul espoir de réussir.

A l'égard du soutien de ses droits, il faut d'abord remarquer qu'une infinité de chicanes et de prétentions obscures et embrouillées seront toutes anéanties par le troisième article de la confédération, qui règle définitivement tous les droits réciproques des souverains alliés sur leur actuelle possession : ainsi toutes les demandes et prétentions possibles deviendront claires à l'avenir, et seront jugées dans la diète, à mesure qu'elles pourront naître. Ajoutez que si l'on attaque mes droits, je dois les soutenir par la même voie : or, on ne peut les attaquer par les armes, sans encourir le ban de la diète ; ce n'est donc pas non plus par les armes que j'ai besoin de les défendre. On doit dire la même chose des injures, des torts, des réparations, et de tous les différents imprévus qui peuvent s'élever entre deux souverains ; et le même pouvoir qui doit défendre leurs droits doit aussi redresser leurs griefs.

Quant au dernier article, la solution saute aux yeux. On voit d'abord que, n'ayant plus d'agresseur à craindre, on n'a plus besoin de traité défensif, et que, comme on n'en sauroit

He no longer has any reason for wishing to weaken a neighbour from whom he has no longer anything to fear, and having no hope of success in such an enterprise, he is under no temptation to attempt it.

As regards maintaining their rights, it must first be said that innumerable obscure quibbles and intricate claims will be completely swept away by the third article of the confederation, which settles definitely all the reciprocal rights of the Allied Sovereigns upon the basis of present possession. Thus all possible demands and claims will become clear for the future, and will be adjudged in the Diet as they arise. Add to this, that if my rights are attacked, I must defend them by the same means. Now they cannot be attacked by arms without incurring the ban of the Diet ; so it is not by arms that I must needs defend them. The same thing can be said of the injuries, wrongs, and reparations, and of all the different unforeseen disputes which might arise between two sovereigns ; the same power which has to defend their rights, has to redress their grievances.

As to the last article the solution is obvious. You can see that having no aggressor to fear there is no need for a defensive treaty, and as no such treaty can be firmer or surer than that of

faire de plus solide et de plus sûr que celui de
la grande confédération, tout autre seroit inutile,
illégitime, et par conséquent nul.

Il n'est donc pas possible que la confédération,
une fois établie, puisse laisser aucune semence de
guerre entre les confédérés, et que l'objet de la
paix perpétuelle ne soit exactement rempli par
l'exécution du systême proposé.

Il nous reste maintenant à examiner l'autre
question, qui regarde l'avantage des parties contractantes ; car on sent bien que vainement
feroit-on parler l'intérêt public au préjudice de
l'intérêt particulier. Prouver que la paix est en
général préférable à la guerre, c'est ne rien dire
à celui qui croit avoir des raisons de préférer la
guerre à la paix ; et lui montrer les moyens
d'établir une paix durable, ce n'est que l'exciter
à s'y opposer.

En effet, dira-t-on, vous ôtez aux souverains
le droit de se faire justice à eux-mêmes, c'est-à-
dire le précieux droit d'être injustes quand il
leur plaît ; vous leur ôtez le pouvoir de s'agrandir
aux dépens de leurs voisins ; vous les faites
renoncer à ces antiques prétentions qui tirent
leur prix de leur obscurité, parcequ'on les étend
avec sa fortune, à cet appareil de puissance et
de terreur dont ils aiment à effrayer le monde,
à cette gloire des conquêtes dont ils tirent leur

the great confederation, any other would be useless, unlawful, and consequently void and worthless.

It is impossible therefore for the confederation once established to leave any seeds of war amongst its members, or for its object of Perpetual Peace not to be perfectly realised by the proposed scheme if it were carried out.

It remains for us now to examine the other question, which concerns the advantage of the contracting parties; for one feels how vain it would be to give the public interest precedence over the private. To prove that peace is generally preferable to war means nothing to whosoever thinks he has reasons for preferring war to peace, and to show him how to establish a lasting peace is only to incite him to oppose it.

In fact, they will say, you take away from Sovereigns the right of doing justice to themselves, that is to say the precious right of being unjust when they please. You take away from them the power of aggrandising themselves at the expense of their neighbours. You make them renounce antiquated claims which owe their value to their obscurity, because they expand them as their fortune warrants; this display of power and terror with which they like to frighten the world, and that pride of conquest from which

F 63

honneur ; et, pour tout dire enfin, vous les
forcez d'être équitables et pacifiques. Quels
seront les dédommagements de tant de cruelles
privations ?

Je n'oserois répondre, avec l'abbé de Saint-
Pierre, que la véritable gloire des princes con-
siste à procurer l'utilité publique et le bonheur
de leurs sujets ; que tous leurs intérêts sont sub-
ordonnés à leur réputation ; et que la réputation
qu'on acquiert auprès des sages se mesure sur le
bien que l'on fait aux hommes ; que l'entreprise
d'une paix perpétuelle, étant la plus grande qui
ait jamais été faite, est la plus capable de couvrir
son auteur d'une gloire immortelle ; que cette
même entreprise, étant aussi la plus utile aux
peuples, est encore la plus honorable aux souverains, la seule sur-tout qui ne soit pas souillée
de sang, de rapines, de pleurs, de malédictions ;
et qu'enfin le plus sûr moyen de se distinguer
dans la foule des rois est de travailler au bonheur
public. Laissons aux harangueurs ces discours
qui, dans les cabinets des ministres, ont couvert
de ridicule l'auteur et ses projets, mais ne
méprisons pas comme eux ses raisons ; et, quoi
qu'il en soit des vertus des princes, parlons de
leurs intérêts.

Toutes les puissances de l'Europe ont des
droits ou des prétentions les unes contre les

they derive their renown; in a word, you force them to be just and peaceable. What will be the compensations for so many cruel deprivations?

I should not be so bold as to reply with the Abbé de Saint-Pierre that the true glory of princes consists in securing the public good and the happiness of their people; that all their interests should be subordinated to their reputation, and that the reputation to be gained among the wise is measured by the good they do to men; that the enterprise of establishing Perpetual Peace, being the greatest undertaking that has ever been conceived, is the most capable of covering its author with immortal glory; that this same enterprise, being on the one hand the most useful to peoples, is on the other the most honourable to sovereigns; and above all it is the only one unsoiled with blood, rapine, tears, and curses. And that finally the surest means of distinguishing oneself amongst the crowd of kings is to work for the public welfare. Let us leave to the speechifiers those discourses which in the cabinets of ministers have covered their author and his project with ridicule, but do not let us, like them, treat his reasons with contempt, and, whatever virtues kings may possess, let us confine ourselves to their interests.

All the Powers of Europe have rights or claims

autres ; ces droits ne sont pas de nature à pouvoir jamais être parfaitement éclaircis, parcequ'il n'y a point, pour en juger, de règle commune et constante, et qu'ils sont souvent fondés sur des faits équivoques ou incertains. Les différents qu'ils causent ne sauroient non plus être jamais terminés sans retour, tant faute d'arbitre compétent, que parceque chaque prince revient dans l'occasion sans scrupule sur les cessions qui lui ont été arrachées par force dans des traités par les plus puissants, ou après des guerres malheureuses. C'est donc une erreur de ne songer qu'à ses prétentions sur les autres, et d'oublier celles des autres sur nous, lorsqu'il n'y a d'aucun côté ni plus de justice ni plus d'avantage dans les moyens de faire valoir ces prétentions réciproques. Sitôt que tout dépend de la fortune, la possession actuelle est d'un prix que la sagesse ne permet pas de risquer contre le profit à venir, même à chance égale ; et tout le monde blâme un homme à son aise qui, dans l'espoir de doubler son bien, l'ose risquer en un coup de dé. Mais nous avons fait voir que, dans les projets d'agrandissement, chacun, même dans le systême actuel, doit trouver une résistance supérieure à son effort ; d'où il suit que les plus puissants n'ayant aucune raison de jouer, ni les plus foibles aucun espoir de profit, c'est un bien pour tous de renoncer

66

one against the other. These rights are not of
such a nature that they can ever be perfectly
cleared up, because there is no common invariable
rule by which to judge them, and they are often
based on ambiguous or uncertain facts. The
disputes they cause could never be ended without
fear of their returning, as much for the want of a
competent arbitrator as because each prince, as
occasion occurs, will not scruple to repudiate those
concessions forced from him in treaties by greater
potentates than himself, or as a result of unsuccessful wars. It is, then, an error to think only
of our own claims on others, and to forget those
of others upon us, when there is no more justice
or advantage on either side in the methods they
use for enforcing these mutual claims. Directly
everything depends on chance, present possession
becomes of such value that prudence will run no
risk of losing it for any future gain, even if the
chances are even ; and everyone condemns a
well-to-do man who, in the hope of doubling his
wealth, dares to risk it on a single throw. But
we have shown that in schemes of aggrandisement
each one, even in the present system, must find
a resistance superior in strength to his own effort ;
whence it follows that the stronger having no
reason to gamble, nor the weaker any hope of
profit, it would be an advantage for all to renounce

67

à ce qu'ils désirent, pour s'assurer ce qu'ils possèdent.

Considérons la consommation d'hommes, d'argent, de forces de toute espèce, l'épuisement où la plus heureuse guerre jette un état quelconque, et comparons ce préjudice aux avantages qu'il en retire ; nous trouverons qu'il perd souvent quand il croit gagner, et que le vainqueur, toujours plus foible qu'avant la guerre, n'a de consolation que de voir le vaincu plus affoibli que lui ; encore cet avantage est-il moins réel qu'apparent, parceque la supériorité qu'on peut avoir acquise sur son adversaire, on l'a perdue en même temps contre les puissances neutres, qui, sans changer d'état, se fortifient, par rapport à nous, de tout notre affoiblissement.

Si tous les rois ne sont pas revenus encore de la folie des conquêtes, il semble au moins que les plus sages commencent à entrevoir qu'elles coûtent quelquefois plus qu'elles ne valent. Sans entrer à cet égard dans mille distinctions qui nous mèneroient trop loin, on peut dire en général qu'un prince qui, pour reculer ses frontières, perd autant de ses anciens sujets qu'il en acquiert de nouveaux, s'affoiblit en s'agrandissant, parcequ'avec un plus grand espace à défendre il n'a pas plus de défenseurs. Or, on ne peut ignorer que, par la manière dont la guerre se fait

what they covet, in order to keep what they already possess.

Let us consider the waste of men, of money of forces of all kinds, and the exhaustion into which the most successful war throws any state, and compare these injuries with the advantages it gains from it. We shall find that it often loses when it thinks it gains, and the victor, always weaker than before the war, has only the consolation of seeing the vanquished more enfeebled than himself. Again that advantage is less real than apparent, because the superiority, which he may have acquired over his adversary, he has at the same time lost in regard to neutral Powers who, without changing their own condition, are relatively strengthened through his enfeeblement.

If all kings do not yet recognise the folly of conquests, it seems at least as if the wiser ones are beginning to understand that conquests sometimes cost more than they are worth. Without going into a thousand distinctions in this matter, which would carry us too far afield, we may say broadly that a prince, who, in order to push forward his frontiers, loses as many of his old subjects as he gains new ones, only weakens himself by this aggrandisement, because with a larger area to defend he has no more men to

aujourd'hui, la moindre dépopulation qu'elle produit est celle qui se fait dans les armées : c'est bien là la perte apparente et sensible ; mais il s'en fait en même temps dans tout l'état une plus grave et plus irréparable que celle des hommes qui meurent, par ceux qui ne naissent pas, par l'augmentation des impôts, par l'interruption du commerce, par la désertion des campagnes, par l'abandon de l'agriculture : ce mal, qu'on n'aperçoit point d'abord, se fait sentir cruellement dans la suite ; et c'est alors qu'on est étonné d'être si foible, pour s'être rendu si puissant.

Ce qui rend encore les conquêtes moins intéressantes, c'est qu'on sait maintenant par quels moyens on peut doubler et tripler sa puissance, non seulement sans étendre son territoire, mais quelquefois en le resserrant, comme fit très sagement l'empereur Adrien. On sait que ce sont les hommes seuls qui font la force des rois ; et c'est une proposition qui découle de ce que je viens de dire, que de deux états qui nourrissent le même nombre d'habitants, celui qui occupe une moindre étendue de terre est réellement le plus puissant. C'est donc par de bonnes lois, par une sage police, par de grandes vues économiques, qu'un souverain judicieux est sûr d'augmenter ses forces sans rien donner au hasard.

defend it with. Now it is well known that as
the result of the way wars are waged to-day the
loss of life is least on the battlefield. It is there
that the loss is most evident and visible, but at
the same time the State suffers much graver and
more irreparable loss than that of the men who
die, by reason of those men who will never be
born, by the increase of taxation, by the interruption of commerce, by deserted countrysides
and abandoned agriculture. This evil, unper-
ceived at first, makes itself cruelly felt later on,
and it is then that a country is astonished to find
itself so weak as the result of having made itself
so powerful.

What makes conquest still less attractive
is that we know now by what means power can
be doubled and trebled, not only without extend-
ing territory but sometimes through restricting
it, as the Emperor Hadrian (11) very wisely did.
We know that men alone make the strength of
kings, and it results from what I have just said
that of two states which support the same number
of inhabitants the one which occupies the least
extent of territory is really the most powerful.
It is then by good laws, by a wise policy, by
broad economic views that a judicious sovereign
is sure of adding to his strength without any
risk. The real conquests he makes over his

Les véritables conquêtes qu'il fait sur ses voisins sont les établissements plus utiles qu'il forme dans ses états ; et tous les sujets de plus qui lui naissent sont autant d'ennemis qu'il tue.

Il ne faut point m'objecter ici que je prouve trop, en ce que, si les choses étoient comme je les représente, chacun ayant un véritable intérêt de ne pas entrer en guerre, et les intérêts particuliers s'unissant à l'intérêt commun pour maintenir la paix, cette paix devroit s'établir d'elle-même et durer toujours sans aucune confédération. Ce seroit faire un fort mauvais raisonnement dans la présente constitution ; car, quoiqu'il fût beaucoup meilleur pour tous d'être toujours en paix, le défaut commun de sûreté à cet égard fait que chacun, ne pouvant s'assurer d'éviter la guerre, tâche au moins de la commencer à son avantage quand l'occasion le favorise, et de prévenir un voisin qui ne manqueroit pas de le prévenir à son tour dans l'occasion contraire ; de sorte que beaucoup de guerres, même offensives, sont d'injustes précautions pour mettre en sûreté son propre bien, plutôt que des moyens d'usurper celui des autres. Quelque salutaires que puissent être généralement les maximes du bien public, il est certain qu'à ne considérer que l'objet qu'on regarde en politique, et souvent même en morale, elles

neighbours are the public improvements he institutes in his domains, and all the additional subjects born to him are worth so many more enemies slain.

It must not be objected here that I prove too much, in that if things were as I represent them, everyone having a genuine interest in not going to war, and private interests being at one with the common interest to maintain peace, this peace would establish itself of itself and last for ever without any confederation. This would be extremely bad reasoning in the present state of things ; for although it would be better for all to be always at peace, the common lack of security in this respect brings it about that each one, not being able to be sure of avoiding war, tries at least to begin it to his own advantage when opportunity favours him, and to forestall a neighbour who would not hesitate to forestall him in the opposite circumstances, so that many wars, even offensive ones, are unjust precautions to safeguard one's own possessions rather than means of seizing what belongs to others. However salutary in general the principles of public welfare may be, it is certain if one considers nothing but the object that he has in view in politics, and often even in morals, these principles become harmful to him who persists in practising

73

deviennent pernicieuses à celui qui s'obstine à les pratiquer avec tout le monde quand personne ne les pratique avec lui.

Je n'ai rien à dire sur l'appareil des armes, parceque, destitué de fondements solides, soit de crainte, soit d'espérance, cet appareil est un jeu d'enfants, et que les rois ne doivent point avoir de poupées. Je ne dis rien non plus de la gloire des conquérants, parceque, s'il y avoit quelques monstres qui s'affligeassent uniquement pour n'avoir personne à massacrer, il ne faudroit point leur parler raison, mais leur ôter les moyens d'exercer leur rage meurtrière. La garantie de l'article troisième ayant prévenu toutes solides raisons de guerre, on ne sauroit avoir de motif de l'allumer contre autrui qui ne puisse en fournir autant à autrui contre nous-mêmes ; et c'est gagner beaucoup que de s'affranchir d'un risque où chacun est seul contre tous.

Quant à la dépendance où chacun sera du tribunal commun, il est très clair qu'elle ne diminuera rien des droits de la souveraineté, mais les affermira, au contraire, et les rendra plus assurés par l'article troisième, en garantissant à chacun, non seulement ses états contre toute invasion étrangère, mais encore son autorité contre toute rébellion de ses sujets. Ainsi les princes n'en seront pas moins absolus, et leur

them towards everyone when no one will practise them towards him.

I have nothing to say about armaments because without a solid basis either of fear or of hope, this outward show is a child's game, and kings should not play with dolls. I say nothing either about the glory of conquerors, because, if there were monsters who were distressed solely because they had no one to massacre, it is no use reasoning with them, but the means of exercising their murderous fury should be taken away from them. The guarantee of the third article having anticipated all sound reasons for war, there could be no motive for kindling war against our neighbours which would not equally apply to their attacking us ; and it is a great gain to be rid of a risk where each one is alone against all.

As to the dependence which each one will be under to the common tribunal, it is very clear that it will diminish none of the rights of sovereignty, but on the contrary will strengthen them, and will make them more assured by article three, which guarantees to each one not only his territory against all foreign invasion, but also his authority against all rebellion by his subjects. The princes accordingly will be none the less absolute, and their crowns will be all the more secure, so that in submitting their disputes to

couronne en sera plus assurée ; de sorte qu'en se soumettant au jugement de la diète dans leurs démêlés d'égal à égal, et s'ôtant le dangereux pouvoir de s'emparer du bien d'autrui, ils ne font que s'assurer de leurs véritables droits et renoncer à ceux qu'ils n'ont pas. D'ailleurs il y a bien de la différence entre dépendre d'autrui ou seulement d'un corps dont on est membre et dont chacun est chef à son tour ; car, en ce dernier cas, on ne fait qu'assurer sa liberté par les garants qu'on lui donne ; elle s'aliéneroit dans les mains d'un maître, mais elle s'affermit dans celles des associés. Ceci se confirme par l'exemple du corps germanique ; car bien que la souveraineté de ses membres soit altérée à bien des égards par sa constitution, et qu'ils soient par conséquent dans un cas moins favorable que ne seroient ceux du corps européen, il n'y en a pourtant pas un seul, quelque jaloux qu'il soit de son autorité, qui voulût, quand il le pourroit, s'assurer une indépendance absolue en se détachant de l'empire.

Remarquez de plus que le corps germanique ayant un chef permanent, l'autorité de ce chef doit nécessairement tendre sans cesse à l'usurpation ; ce qui ne peut arriver de même dans la diète européenne, où la présidence doit être alternative et sans égard à l'inégalité de puissance.

the judgment of the Diet as among equals, and renouncing the dangerous power of seizing the possessions of others they only make sure of their true rights and give up those which do not belong to them. Moreover there is a great deal of difference between being dependent on one's neighbours or only on a body of which one is a member, and of which each one is the head in his turn, for in this last case his liberty is only ensured by the guarantees that are given to him. It would be alienated in the hands of a master, but is confirmed in the hands of associates. This is proved by the example of the Germanic States, for although the sovereignty of its members may be weakened in many respects by its constitution, and so they are in a less favourable position than the states of the European body would be, there is nevertheless not a single one of them, however jealous it may be of its own authority, who would wish, when it could, to assure itself an absolute independence by detaching itself from the empire.

Mark further that as the German States have a permanent head, the authority of this head must necessarily and unceasingly tend to become arbitrary, which could not happen in the same way under the European Diet, where the Presidency would rotate without regard to disparity of power.

A toutes ces considérations il s'en joint une
autre bien plus importante encore pour des
gens aussi avides d'argent que le sont toujours
les princes ; c'est une grande facilité de plus d'en
avoir beaucoup par tous les avantages qui résul-
teront pour leurs peuples et pour eux d'une paix
continuelle, et par l'excessive dépense qu'épargne
la réforme de l'état militaire, de ces multitudes
de forteresses et de cette énorme quantité de
troupes qui absorbe leurs revenus, et devient
chaque jour plus à charge à leurs peuples et à
eux-mêmes. Je sais qu'il ne convient pas à tous
les souverains de supprimer toutes leurs troupes,
et de n'avoir aucune force publique en main
pour étouffer une émeute inopinée, ou repousser
une invasion subite.* Je sais encore qu'il y aura
un contingent à fournir à la confédération, tant
pour la garde des frontières de l'Europe que
pour l'entretien de l'armée confédérative destinée
à soutenir au besoin les décrets de la diète.
Mais toutes ces dépenses faites, et l'extraordinaire
des guerres à jamais supprimé, il resteroit encore
plus de la moitié de la dépense militaire ordinaire
à répartir entre le soulagement des sujets et

---

* Il se présente encore ici d'autres objections ; mais, comme
l'auteur du Projet ne se les est pas faites, je les ai rejetées
dans l'examen.

To all these considerations another is added
more potent still to persons as eager for money
as princes always are. I mean the advantage
of having much more of it ; for great wealth
would accrue to their people and to themselves
from a continual peace, from the enormous
saving effected by the reduction of the military
establishment with a multitude of fortresses and
an enormous quantity of troops, which swallow
up their revenues and become daily a heavier
charge on their people and themselves. I know
it would not be well for all sovereigns to disband
all their troops and not to have any standing
public force to stifle an unexpected rising or
repulse a sudden invasion.* I know too that a
contingent will have to be furnished for the
Confederation, both for the defence of the
frontiers of Europe and for the upkeep of the
confederative army which is intended to uphold
when necessary the decrees of the Diet. But
when all these expenses have been met and the
extraordinary expenses of war have been suppressed for ever, there would still remain more
than half of the ordinary military expenditure to
distribute between the relief of the subject and

* Other objections present themselves ; but as the author
of the project has not brought them forward, I have postponed
them until my criticisms.

les coffres du prince : de sorte que le peuple paieroit beaucoup moins ; que le prince, beaucoup plus riche, seroit en état d'exciter le commerce, l'agriculture, les arts, de faire des établissements utiles qui augmenteroient encore la richesse du peuple et la sienne ; et que l'état seroit avec cela dans une sûreté beaucoup plus parfaite que celle qu'il peut tirer de ses armées et de tout cet appareil de guerre qui ne cesse de l'épuiser au sein de la paix.

On dira peut-être que les pays frontières de l'Europe seroient alors dans une position plus désavantageuse, et pourroient avoir également des guerres à soutenir, ou avec le Turc, ou avec les corsaires d'Afrique, ou avec les Tartares.

A cela je réponds, 1° que ces pays sont dans le même cas aujourd'hui, et que par conséquent ce ne seroit pas pour eux un désavantage positif à citer, mais seulement un avantage de moins et un inconvénient inévitable auquel leur situation les expose ; 2° que, délivrés de toute inquiétude du côté de l'Europe, ils seroient beaucoup plus en état de résister au-dehors ; 3° que la suppression de toutes les forteresses de l'intérieur de l'Europe et des frais nécessaires à leur entretien mettroit la confédération en état d'en établir un grand nombre sur les frontières sans être à charge

the coffers of the prince ; so that the people
would pay much less, whilst the prince, being
much richer, would be in a position to encourage
commerce, agriculture and the Arts, and to
found useful institutions which would further
increase the wealth of his people as well as his
own, and the State would be in a much more
perfect state of safety than it could obtain by
means of its armies and all that machinery of
war which is incessantly exhausting it in the midst
of peace.

It may be said perhaps that the frontier
countries of Europe would then be in a more
disadvantageous position and might have all the
same to sustain wars with the Turks, the Corsairs
of Africa, or with the Tartars.

To that I reply : (1) That these countries are
in the very same position to-day, and consequently it should not be quoted as a positive
disadvantage to them, but only as one advantage
the less, and an inevitable inconvenience to
which their situation exposes them. (2) That,
delivered from all anxiety on the European side,
they would be in a much better position to resist
outsiders. (3) That the suppression of all the
fortresses of the interior of Europe and the cost
of keeping them up would make it possible for
the Confederation to establish a large number on

aux confédérés ; 4° que ces forteresses, construites, entretenues et gardées à frais communs, seroient autant de sûretés et de moyens d'épargne pour les puissances frontières dont elles garantiroient les états ; 5° que les troupes de la confédération, distribuées sur les confins de l'Europe, seroient toujours prêtes à repousser l'agresseur ; 6° qu'enfin un corps aussi redoutable que la république européenne ôteroit aux étrangers l'envie d'attaquer aucun de ses membres, comme le corps germanique, infiniment moins puissant, ne laisse pas de l'être assez pour se faire respecter de ses voisins et protéger utilement tous les princes qui le composent.

On pourra dire encore que les Européens n'ayant plus de guerres entre eux, l'art militaire tomberoit insensiblement dans l'oubli ; que les troupes perdroient leur courage et leur discipline ; qu'il n'y auroit plus ni généraux, ni soldats, et que l'Europe resteroit à la merci du premier venu.

Je réponds qu'il arrivera de deux choses l'une : ou les voisins de l'Europe l'attaqueront et lui feront la guerre, ou ils redouteront la confédération et la laisseront en paix.

Dans le premier cas, voilà les occasions de cultiver le génie et les talents militaires, d'aguerrir

the frontiers without expense to the confederates. (4) That these fortresses, constructed, kept up, and garrisoned at the common expense, would be so many pledges and means of economy for the frontier powers whose territories they would defend. (5) That the troops of the Confederation, distributed on the borders of Europe, would always be ready to repulse the aggressor. (6) That finally a body as formidable as the European Republic would take away from foreign countries the desire to attack any of its members, as the Germanic body, infinitely less powerful, is still enough so to make itself respected by its neighbours and usefully to protect all those princes who belong to it.

Again, it might be said that, if Europeans had no more wars among themselves, the art of war would fall gradually into oblivion, that the troops would lose their courage and their discipline, that there would be no more generals or soldiers, and that Europe would lie at the mercy of the first comer.

My reply is that one of two things would happen : either Europe's neighbours would attack and make war on her, or they would be afraid of the Confederation and leave her in peace.

In the first case here are chances for cultivating

et former des troupes ; les armées de la confédération seront à cet egard l'école de l'Europe ;
on ira sur la frontière apprendre la guerre ; dans
le sein de l'Europe on jouira de la paix ; et l'on
réunira par ce moyen les avantages de l'une et
de l'autre. Croit-on qu'il soit toujours nécessaire de se battre chez soi pour devenir guerrier ?
et les François sont-ils moins braves parceque
les provincès de Touraine et d'Anjou ne sont
pas en guerre l'une contre l'autre ?

Dans le second cas, on ne pourra plus s'aguerrir,
il est vrai ; mais on n'en aura plus besoin ; car
à quoi bon s'exercer à la guerre pour ne la
faire à personne ? Lequel vaut mieux de cultiver
un art funeste ou de le rendre inutile ? S'il y
avoit un secret pour jouir d'une santé inaltérable,
y auroit-il du bon sens à le rejeter pour ne pas
ôter aux médecins l'occasion d'acquérir de
l'expérience ? Il reste à voir dans ce parallèle
lequel des deux arts est plus salutaire en soi, et
mérite mieux d'être conservé.

Qu'on ne nous menace pas d'une invasion
subite ; on sait bien que l'Europe n'en a point à
craindre, et que ce premier venu ne viendra
jamais. Ce n'est plus le temps de ces éruptions

military talent and genius and for training and forming the troops. The armies of the confederation would be in this respect the school of Europe. They would go to the frontier to learn about war; peace would reign in the heart of Europe; and by this means the advantages of both would be combined. ∖ Does anyone think that it is always necessary to be fighting at home to become warlike ? Are Frenchmen less brave because the provinces of Touraine and Anjou do not make war on one another ?

In the second case it is true that there would be no more training for war, but there would be no need. Why be trained for fighting if there is no one to fight ? Which is the better, to cultivate a noxious art or to render it unnecessary ? If a secret prescription for the enjoyment of perpetual health were available would there be any sense in rejecting it on the ground that it would deprive doctors of opportunities for gaining experience ? This parallel helps us to see which of the two arts is the more beneficial in itself, and which best deserves to be kept up.

Let them not threaten us with sudden invasion ; we know very well Europe has none to fear, and that this " first comer " will never come. The days have gone by when irruptions of barbarians

de barbares qui sembloient tombés des nues.
Depuis que nous parçourons d'un œil curieux
toute la surface de la terre, il ne peut plus rien
venir jusqu'à nous qui ne soit prevu de tres
loin. Il n'y a nulle puissance au monde qui soit
maintenant en état de menacer l'Europe entière ;
et si jamais il en vient une, ou l'on aura le temps
de se préparer, ou l'on sera du moins plus en
état de lui resister, étant unis en un corps, que
quand il faudra terminer tout d'un coup de longs
différents et se réunir à la hâte.

Nous venons de voir que tous les prétendus
inconvénients de l'état de confédération bien
pesés se réduisent à rien. Nous demandons
maintenant si quelqu'un dans le monde en
oseroit dire autant de ceux qui résultent de
la manière actuelle de vider les différents entre
prince et prince par le droit du plus fort, c'est-à-
dire de l'état d'impolice et de guerre qu'engendre
nécessairement l'indépendance absolue et mutuelle
de tous les souverains dans la société imparfaite
qui règne entre eux dans l'Europe. Pour qu'on
soit mieux en état de peser ces inconvénients,
j'en vais résumer en peu de mots le sommaire
que je laisse examiner au lecteur.

1. Nul droit assuré que celui du plus fort.
2. Changements continuels et inévitables de
relations entre les peuples, qui empêchent aucun

seemed to fall from the clouds. Ever since we have been able to cast an inquiring eye over the surface of the earth nothing can reach us which cannot be foreseen at a great distance. (There is no power in the world which is now in a state to threaten the whole of Europe, and if one should ever arise, either there would be time to prepare, or at least we should be in a better state to resist it being united in one body, than if it were necessary suddenly to end long-standing quarrels and reunite in haste.

We have just seen that all the pretended inconveniences of the confederative state, when well weighed, come to nothing. We now ask if anyone in the world would dare to say as much of those inconveniences which result from the present method of settling differences between prince and prince by the right of the strongest, that is to say of the state of uncivilization and war which the absolute and mutual independence of all the sovereigns, in the imperfect society which reigns amongst them in Europe, necessarily engenders. That the reader may be in a better position to weigh these inconveniences I am going to sum them up in a few words which I shall leave him to investigate.

(1) No rights assured but those of the strongest.
(2) Continual and inevitable changes in the

d'eux de pouvoir fixer en ses mains la force dont il jouit. 3. Point de sûreté parfaite, aussi long-temps que les voisins ne sont pas soumis ou anéantis. 4. Impossibilité générale de les anéantir, attendu qu'en subjuguant les premiers on en trouve d'autres. 5. Précautions et frais immenses pour se tenir sur ses gardes. 6. Défaut de force et de défense dans les minorités et dans les révoltes ; car quand l'état se partage, qui peut soutenir un des partis contre l'autre ? 7. Défaut de sûreté dans les engagements mutuels. 8. Jamais de justice à espérer d'autrui sans des frais et des pertes immenses, qui ne l'obtiennent pas toujours, et dont l'objet disputé ne dédommage que rarement. 9. Risque inévitable de ses états et quelquefois de sa vie dans la poursuite de ses droits. 10. Nécessité de prendre part malgré soi aux querelles de ses voisins, et d'avoir la guerre quand on la voudroit le moins. 11. Interruption du commerce et des ressources publiques au moment qu'elles sont le plus nécessaires. 12. Danger continuel de la part d'un voisin puissant si l'on est foible, et d'une ligue si l'on est fort. 13. Enfin inutilité de la sagesse où préside la fortune ; désolation continuelle des peuples ;

88

relations between the nations, which prevent anyone of them from retaining in its hands the power that it enjoys. (3) No perfect security so long as neighbours are not subdued or annihilated. (4) The general impossibility of reducing them to helplessness, seeing that while one enemy is being subjugated others appear on the scene. (5) Immense precautions and expense in always being in a state of defence. (6) Lack of power of defence during minorities and rebellions, for when the state is divided who can support one of the parties against the other? (7) Unreliability of mutual pledges.' (8) No hope of justice from others without immense expenses and losses which do not always obtain it, and for which the matter in dispute when gained seldom compensates. (9) The inevitable risking of one's territories and sometimes of one's life in pursuit of one's rights. (10) The necessity in spite of one's self of taking part in the quarrels of one's neighbours and of making war when one least desires it. (11) The interruption of commerce and the public revenues at the moment when they are most needful. (12) The continual danger from a powerful neighbour if one is weak, and from a coalition if one is strong. (13) Finally, the uselessness of wisdom where fortune holds sway; the continual distress of nations; enfeeble-

affoiblissement de l'état dans les succès et dans les revers ; impossibilité totale d'établir jamais un bon gouvernement, de compter sur son propre bien, et de rendre heureux ni soi ni les autres.

Récapitulons de même les avantages de l'arbitrage européen pour les princes confédérés.

1. Sûreté entière que leurs différents présents et futurs seront toujours terminés sans aucune guerre ; sûreté incomparablement plus utile pour eux que ne seroit, pour les particuliers, celle de n'avoir jamais de procès.

2. Sujets de contestations ôtés ou réduits à très peu de chose par l'anéantissement de toutes prétentions antérieures, qui compensera les renonciations et affermira les possessions.

3. Sûreté entière et perpétuelle, et de la personne du prince, et de sa famille, et de ses états, et de l'ordre de succession fixé par les lois de chaque pays, tant contre l'ambition des prétendants injustes et ambitieux, que contre les révoltes des sujets rebelles.

4. Sûreté parfaite de l'exécution de tous les engagements réciproques entre prince et prince, par la garantie de la république européenne.

5. Liberté et sûreté parfaite et perpétuelle à

ment of the state both in successes and reverses ; complete impossibility of ever establishing a good government, counting on one's own possessions or making either one's self or others happy.

Let us also recapitulate the advantages of European arbitration for the princes of the confederation.

(1) A complete assurance that their present and future quarrels will always be terminated without war ; an assurance incomparably more useful to them than that of never having lawsuits would be to an individual.

(2) Matters of dispute eliminated or reduced to a very small compass by the cancellation of all bygone claims which will compensate the nation for what they give up and confirm them in what they possess.

(3) Entire and perpetual security of the person of the prince and of his family and of his territories and of the order of succession fixed by the laws of each country, both against the presumption of unjust and ambitious pretenders and against the revolts of rebel subjects.

(4) Perfect certainty of the execution of all reciprocal engagements between prince and prince by the guarantee of the European Commonwealth.

(5) Perfect and perpetual liberty and security

l'égard du commerce, tant d'état à état, que de chaque état dans les régions éloignées.

6. Suppression totale et perpétuelle de leur dépense militaire extraordinaire par terre et par mer en temps de guerre, et considérable diminution de leur dépense ordinaire en temps de paix.

7. Progrès sensible de l'agriculture et de la population, des richesses de l'état, et des revenus du prince.

8. Facilité de tous les établissements qui peuvent augmenter la gloire et l'autorité du souverain, les ressources publiques et le bonheur des peuples.

Je laisse, comme je l'ai déjà dit, au jugement des lecteurs l'examen de tous ces articles, et la comparaison de l'état de paix qui résulte de la confédération, avec l'état de guerre qui résulte de l'impolice européenne.

Si nous avons bien raisonné dans l'exposition de ce projet, il est démontré premièrement que l'établissement de la paix perpétuelle dépend uniquement du consentement des souverains, et n'offre point à lever d'autre difficulté que leur résistance ; secondement, que cet établissement leur seroit utile de toute manière, et qu'il n'y a nulle comparaison à faire, même pour eux, entre les inconvénients et les avantages ; en troisième

of trade, both between state and state and for each state in distant lands.

(6) Total and perpetual suppression of their extraordinary military expenditure by land and by sea in time of war, and considerable diminution of their ordinary expenditure in time of peace.

(7) A marked progress in agriculture and population, in the wealth of the state, and in the revenues of the prince.

(8) An opportunity for the promotion of all the institutions which can increase the glory and authority of the sovereign, the public resources, and the happiness of the people.

I leave as I have already said to the judgment of my readers the examination of all these articles, and the comparison of the state of peace which results from the confederation, with the state of war which results from the unsettled constitution of Europe.

If we have reasoned logically in the statement of this project, it has been demonstrated, first, that the establishment of perpetual peace wholly depends on the consent of sovereigns, and raises no other difficulty than their resistance to it ; secondly, that this establishment would be useful to them in every way, and that even for the princes there is no comparison between the disadvantages and the advantages ; in the third

lieu, qu'il est raisonnable de supposer que leur volonté s'accorde avec leur intérêt ; enfin que cet établissement, une fois formé sur le plan proposé, seroit solide et durable, et rempliroit parfaitement son objet. Sans doute ce n'est pas à dire que les souverains adopteront ce projet, (qui peut répondre de la raison d'autrui ?) mais seulement qu'ils l'adopteroient s'ils consultoient leurs vrais intérêts : car on doit bien remarquer que nous n'avons point supposé les hommes tels qu'ils devroient être, bons, généreux, désinté-ressés, et aimant le bien public par humanité ; mais tels qu'ils sont, injustes, avides, et préférant leur intérêt à tout. La seule chose qu'on leur suppose, c'est assez de raison pour voir ce qui leur est utile, et assez de courage pour faire leur propre bonheur. Si, malgré tout cela, ce projet demeure sans exécution, ce n'est donc pas qu'il soit chimérique ; c'est que les hommes sont insensés, et que c'est une sorte de folie d'être sage au milieu des fous.

place, that it is reasonable to suppose that their wishes accord with their interests; and lastly that this institution once formed on the proposed plan, would be solid and durable, and would perfectly fulfil its object.

Certainly it does not follow that the sovereigns would adopt this project (who can answer for other people's intelligence?) but only that they would adopt it if they consulted their true interests; for the reader must observe that (we have not supposed men to be such as they ought to be—good, generous, disinterested, and loving public good from motives of human sympathy— but such as they are, unjust, greedy, and preferring their own interests to everything else. The only thing we assume on their behalf is enough intelligence to see what is useful to themselves, and enough courage to achieve their own happiness. ⟍ If, in spite of all this, this project is not carried into execution, it is not because it is chimerical, it is because men are crazy and because to be sane in the midst of madmen is a sort of folly.

JUGEMENT SUR LA PAIX
PERPETUELLE

LE projet de la paix perpétuelle, étant par son
objet le plus digne d'occuper un homme de
bien, fut aussi de tous ceux de l'abbé de Saint-
Pierre celui qu'il médita le plus long-temps et
qu'il suivit avec le plus d'opiniâtreté ; car on a
peine à nommer autrement ce zèle de mission-
naire qui ne l'abandonna jamais sur ce point,
malgré l'évidente impossibilité du succès, le
ridicule qu'il se donnoit de jour en jour, et les
dégoûts qu'il eut sans cesse à essuyer. Il semble
que cette âme saine, uniquement attentive au
bien public, mesuroit les soins qu'elle donnoit
aux choses uniquement sur le degré de leur
utilité, sans jamais se laisser rebuter par les
obstacles ni songer à l'intérêt personnel.

Si jamais vérité morale fut démontrée, il me
semble que c'est l'utilité générale et particulière
de ce projet. Les avantages qui résulteroient de
son exécution, et pour chaque prince, et pour
chaque peuple, et pour toute l'Europe, sont
immenses, clairs, incontestables ; on ne peut rien
de plus solide et de plus exact que les raisonne-

JUDGMENT ON PERPETUAL PEACE

THE project of a perpetual peace, considering its object one of the most worthy to engage a man of high ideals, was, of all those entertained by the Abbé de Saint-Pierre, the one which he meditated the longest and pursued with the most obstinacy. For it is difficult to speak otherwise of the missionary ardour which never forsook him on this subject, in spite of the evident impossibility of success, the daily ridicule to which he exposed himself, and the mortifications he had constantly to bear. It seems as though his pure heart, intent only upon the public welfare, measured the care he bestowed on a cause solely by the degree of its usefulness, never allowing him to be discouraged by obstacles and never dreaming of personal advantage.

If ever a moral truth was demonstrated, it seems to me it is the general and special utility of this project. The advantages which would accrue to every prince, to every people and to the whole of Europe, from its practical adoption, are immense, obvious, undeniable. Nothing

ments par lesquels l'auteur les établit. Réalisez
sa république européenne durant un seul jour,
c'en est assez pour la faire durer éternellement,
tant chacun trouveroit par l'expérience son profit
particulier dans le bien commun. Cependant ces
mêmes princes qui la défendroient de toutes leurs
forces si elle existoit, s'opposeroient maintenant
de même à son exécution, et l'empêcheront
infailliblement de s'établir comme ils l'em-
pêcheroient de s'éteindre. Ainsi l'ouvrage de
l'abbé de Saint-Pierre sur la paix perpétuelle
paroît d'abord inutile pour la produire et
superflu pour la conserver. C'est donc une vaine
spéculation, dira quelque lecteur impatient. Non,
c'est un livre solide et sensé, et il est très important
qu'il existe.

Commençons par examiner les difficultés de
ceux qui ne jugent pas des raisons par la raison,
mais seulement par l'événement, et qui n'ont
rien à objecter contre ce projet, sinon qu'il n'a
pas été exécuté. En effet, diront-ils sans doute,
si ses avantages sont si réels, pourquoi donc les
souverains de l'Europe ne l'ont-ils pas adopté ?
pourquoi négligent-ils leur propre intérêt, si cet
intérêt leur est si bien démontré ? Voit-on qu'ils

could be more consistent or more true than the reasoning by which the author sets them forth. Realise his European Commonwealth for a single day; and the experience would be enough to make it last for ever, so much would every one realise his own advantage in the common good. But these same princes who would defend it with all their might if it existed, would all the same oppose its introduction now, and would prevent its establishment as infallibly as they would hinder its destruction. Thus the work of the Abbé de Saint-Pierre appears at first sight ineffectual for the purpose of establishing a perpetual peace and superfluous for preserving it. "It is therefore a vain speculation," some impatient reader will say. No; it is a solid, sensible book and its existence is very important indeed.

Let us begin by examining the difficulties of those who do not judge reasons by reason but only by results, and have nothing to object to in the project except that it has not been put into practice. As a matter of fact, no doubt they will say, if its advantages are so real, why then have the sovereigns of Europe not adopted it? Why do they neglect their own interests, when those interests have been so thoroughly demonstrated to them? Do we see these

rejettent d'ailleurs les moyens d'augmenter leurs revenus et leur puissance ? Si celui-ci étoit aussi bon pour cela qu'on le prétend, est-il croyable qu'ils en fussent moins empressés que de tous ceux qui les égarent depuis si long-temps, et qu'ils préférassent mille ressources trompeuses à un profit évident ?

Sans doute cela est croyable ; à moins qu'on ne suppose que leur sagesse est égale à leur ambition, et qu'ils voient d'autant mieux leurs avantages qu'ils les désirent plus fortement ; au lieu que c'est la grande punition des excès de l'amour-propre de recourir toujours à des moyens qui l'abusent, et que l'ardeur même des passions est presque toujours ce qui les détourne de leur but. Distinguons donc, en politique ainsi qu'en morale, l'intérêt réel de l'intérêt apparent : le premier se trouveroit dans la paix perpétuelle ; cela est démontré dans le projet ; le second se trouve dans l'état d'indépendance absolue qui soustrait les souverains à l'empire de la loi pour les soumettre à celui de la fortune. Semblables à un pilote insensé, qui, pour faire montre d'un vain savoir et commander à ses matelots, aimeroit mieux flotter entre des rochers durant la tempête, que d'assujettir son vaisseau par des ancres.

Toute l occupation des rois, ou de ceux qu'ils

sovereigns rejecting in other ways the means of increasing their revenues or power ? If this means were as valuable as it pretends to be, is it believable that they would be less eager about it than about all those others that have misled them so long ; or that they would prefer a thousand deceptive expedients to such an obvious gain ?

No doubt so we shall believe, unless we suppose that their wisdom is equal to their ambition, and that the more strongly they desire their own interests, the better they discern them ; whereas the great punishment of excessive self-love is always that it overreaches itself, and it is the very fury of a passion that almost always diverts it from its goal. In politics therefore, as in morals, let us distinguish real from apparent interests. The first would be found in Perpetual Peace ; that is shewn by the project. The second is to be found in the state of absolute independence which removes sovereigns from the reign of law and submits them to that of chance. They resemble a vain and headstrong pilot who, to show off his empty skill and authority over his sailors, would rather drift to and fro among the rocks during a storm, than let his vessel lie at anchor.

All the business of kings or of those to whom they delegate their duties, is concerned with two

chargent de leurs fonctions, se rapporte à deux
seuls objets, étendre leur domination au-dehors,
et la rendre plus absolue au-dedans : toute autre
vue, ou se rapporte à l'une de ces deux, ou ne
leur sert que de prétexte ; telles sont celles du
bien public, du *bonheur des sujets*, de la *gloire
de la nation ;* mots à jamais proscrits du cabinet,
et si lourdement employés dans les édits publics,
qu'ils n'annoncent jamais que des ordres funestes,
et que le peuple gémit d'avance quand ses
maîtres lui parlent de leurs soins paternels.

Qu'on juge, sur ces deux maximes fondamentales, comment les princes peuvent recevoir une
proposition qui choque directement l'une, et
qui n'est guère plus favorable à l'autre. Car
on sent bien que par la diète européenne le
gouvernement de chaque état n'est pas moins
fixé que par ses limites, qu'on ne peut garantir
les princes de la révolte des sujets sans garantir
en même temps les sujets de la tyrannie des
princes, et qu'autrement l'institution ne sauroit subsister. Or, je demande s'il y a dans le
monde un seul souverain qui, borné ainsi pour
jamais dans ses projets les plus chéris, supportât
sans indignation la seule idée de se voir forcé
d'être juste, non seulement avec les étrangers,
mais même avec ses propres sujets.

objects alone ; to extend their rule abroad or to make it more absolute at home. Any other view is either subservient to one of these objects, or a mere pretext for obtaining them. Such are the " public good," " the welfare of the people," or the " glory of the nation " ; words always banished from the king's closet, and so clumsily used in public edicts that they only seem to be warnings of approaching misery ; and the people groan in advance when their masters speak to them of their paternal care.

Let anyone judge from these two fundamental maxims how princes might take a proposal which directly clashes with one and is scarcely more favourable to the other. For anyone can see that by the establishment of this European Diet the government of each state is fixed as rigidly as its frontiers ; and that no prince can be guaranteed against the revolt of his subjects unless at the same time the subjects are guaranteed against the tyranny of the prince ; on no other terms could the institution be maintained. Now I ask whether there is a single sovereign in the world who, thus restrained forever from engaging in his most cherished schemes, would bear without indignation the mere idea of seeing himself forced to be just, not only to foreigners, but even to his own subjects.

Il est facile encore de comprendre que d'un côté la guerre et les conquêtes, et de l'autre les progrès du despotisme, s'entr'aident mutuellement ; qu'on prend à discrétion, dans un peuple d'esclaves, de l'argent et des hommes pour en subjuguer d'autres ; que réciproquement la guerre fournit un prétexte aux exactions pécuniaires, et un autre non moins spécieux d'avoir toujours de grandes armées pour tenir le peuple en respect. Enfin chacun voit assez que les princes conquérants font pour le moins autant la guerre à leurs sujets qu'à leurs ennemis, et que la condition des vainqueurs n'est pas meilleure que celle des vaincus. *J'ai battu les Romains*, écrivoit Annibal aux Cathaginois ; *envoyez-moi des troupes : j'ai mis l'Italie à contribution, envoyez-moi de l'argent.* Voilà ce que signifient les *Te Deum*, les feux de joie, et l'alégresse du peuple aux triomphes de ses maîtres.

Quant aux différents entre prince et prince, peut-on espérer de soumettre à un tribunal supérieur des hommes qui s'osent vanter de ne tenir leur pouvoir que de leur épée, et qui ne font mention de Dieu même que parcequ'il est au ciel ? Les souverains se soumettront-ils dans leurs querelles à des voies juridiques, que toute la rigueur des lois n'a jamais pu forcer les particuliers d'admettre dans les leurs ? Un simple

It is easy of course to understand how war and conquests assist the development of despotism and vice versa ; from a people of slaves you can take as much money and as many men as you please to subjugate others ; and war furnishes in turn a pretext for taxation, and another, no less specious, for keeping large armies to hold the people in awe. In a word, everyone sees well enough that conquering princes make war at least as much on their subjects as on their enemies, and that the condition of the victors is no better than that of the vanquished. " I have beaten the Romans," wrote Hannibal to the Carthaginians. " Send me troops : I have taxed Italy, send me money." This is the meaning of the Te Deums, fireworks, and the huzzas of the people at the triumph of their masters.

As to the quarrels between prince and prince, can one hope to compel men to submit to a superior tribunal, who dare to boast that they hold their power by the sword alone, and refer to God Himself only because He is in heaven ? Will quarrelling sovereigns submit themselves to judicial methods, when all the rigour of the law has never been able to force private individuals to bow to justice ? A private gentleman, with a grievance, disdains to carry it before a Court

gentilhomme offensé dédaigne de porter ses plaintes au tribunal des maréchaux de France ; et vous voulez qu'un roi porte les siennes à la diète européenne ? Encore y a-t-il cette différence, que l'un pèche contre les lois et expose doublement sa vie, au lieu que l'autre n'expose guère que ses sujets ; qu'il use, en prenant les armes, d'un droit avoué de tout le genre humain, et dont il prétend n'être comptable qu'à Dieu seul.

Un prince qui met sa cause au hasard de la guerre n'ignore pas qu'il court des risques ; mais il en est moins frappé que des avantages qu'il se promet, parcequ'il craint bien moins la fortune qu'il n'espère de sa propre sagesse : s'il est puissant, il compte sur ses forces ; s'il est foible, il compte sur ses alliances ; quelquefois il lui est utile au-dedans de purger de mauvaises humeurs, d'affoiblir des sujets indociles, d'essuyer même des revers, et le politique habile sait tirer avantage de ses propres défaites. J'espère qu'on se souviendra que ce n'est pas moi qui raisonne ainsi, mais le sophiste de cour, qui préfère un grand territoire et peu de sujets pauvres et soumis, à l'empire inébranlable que donnent au prince la justice et les lois sur un peuple heureux et florissant.

C'est encore par le même principe qu'il réfute

of the Marshals of France, and you want a king to take his before a Diet of Europe ? Again there is this difference, that the former is breaking the law and so risking his life twice, while the other risks only the life of his subjects ; and in taking up arms he is availing himself of a right recognised by all the human race, and one for which he claims to be responsible to God alone.

A prince who puts his cause to the hazard of war well knows that he is running risks, but he is less conscious of that than of the advantages that he looks to obtain, for he hopes to gain much more from his own wisdom than he fears to lose at the hands of Fortune. If he is powerful he trusts to his troops ; if he is weak he trusts to alliances ; sometimes it is useful to him at home to purge bad humours from within ; to weaken intractable subjects ; even to suffer reverses ; and the clever politician knows how to take advantage of his own very defeats. I hope it will be remembered that it is not I who reason in this way, but the court sophist, who prefers a large territory and a few poor submissive subjects, to the unshakable empire over a happy and prosperous people which comes to princes through the observance of justice and law.

It is again on the same principle that he refutes in his own mind arguments drawn from

en lui-même l'argument tiré de la suspension du commerce, de la dépopulation, du dérangement des finances, et des pertes réelles que cause une vaine conquête. C'est un calcul très fautif que d'évaluer toujours en argent les gains ou les pertes des souverains ; le degré de puissance qu'ils ont en vue ne se compte point par les millions qu'on possède. Le prince fait toujours circuler ses projets ; il veut commander pour s'enrichir, et s'enrichir pour commander ; il sacrifiera tour-à-tour l'un et l'autre pour acquérir celui des deux qui lui manque : mais ce n'est qu'afin de parvenir à les posséder enfin tous les deux ensemble qu'il les poursuit séparément ; car, pour être le maître des hommes et des choses, il faut qu'il ait à-la-fois l'empire et l'argent.

Ajoutons enfin, sur les grands avantages qui doivent résulter, pour le commerce, d'une paix générale et perpétuelle, qu'ils sont bien en eux-mêmes certains et incontestables, mais qu'étant communs à tous ils ne seront réels pour personne, attendu que de tels avantages ne se sentent que par leurs différences, et que, pour augmenter sa puissance relative, on ne doit chercher que des biens exclusifs.

Sans cesse abusés par l'apparence des choses, les princes rejetteroient donc cette paix, quand ils pèseroient leurs intérêts eux-mêmes : que

the suspension of commerce, from depopulation, from the derangement of the finances, and from the real losses that ensue on a useless conquest. It is a great error always to value the gains and losses of sovereigns in money; the amount of power they aim at is not measured by the millions of money they possess. The prince always makes his plans rotate; he wants to rule in order to enrich himself, and to enrich himself in order to rule; he will sacrifice by turns the one aim to the other in order to gain whichever of the two is wanting; but it is only in order to succeed at last in possessing both together, that he pursues them separately; for to be the master of men and affairs he must have at one and the same time power and money.

Let us add for a final argument that although it is certain that the advantages which should result to commerce from a general and Perpetual Peace would be great, yet, being common to all, they would be realised by none, seeing that such advantages are only felt by contrast, and that to increase one's power in relation to others, one ought to seek only exclusive gains.

Imposed on constantly by appearances, princes would therefore reject this Peace, even if they weighed their own interests themselves; what would it be like when they let these interests be

sera-ce quand ils les feront peser par leurs ministres, dont les intérêts sont toujours opposés à
ceux du peuple et presque toujours à ceux du
prince ? Les ministres ont besoin de la guerre
pour se rendre nécessaires, pour jeter le prince
dans des embarras dont il ne se puisse tirer sans
eux, et pour perdre l'état, s'il le faut, plutôt
que leur place ; ils en ont besoin pour vexer le
peuple sous prétexte des nécessités publiques ;
ils en ont besoin pour placer leurs créatures,
gagner sur les marchés, et faire en secret mille
odieux monopoles ; ils en ont besoin pour satis-
faire leurs passions, et s'expulser mutuellement ;
ils en ont besoin pour s'emparer du prince en le
tirant de la cour quand il s'y forme contre eux
des intrigues dangereuses : ils perdroient toutes
ces ressources par la paix perpétuelle. Et le public
ne laisse pas de demander pourquoi, si ce projet
est possible, ils ne l'ont pas adopté ! Il ne voit
pas qu'il n'y a rien d'impossible dans ce projet,
sinon qu'il soit adopté par eux. Que feront-ils
donc pour s'y opposer ? ce qu'ils ont toujours
fait ; ils le tourneront en ridicule.

Il ne faut pas non plus croire avec l'abbé de
Saint-Pierre que, même avec la bonne volonté
que les princes ni leurs ministres n'auront jamais,
il fût aisé de trouver un moment favorable à

weighed by their ministers, whose own interests
are always opposed to those of the people, and
almost always to those of the prince ? The
ministers want war to make themselves indispensable, to involve the prince in difficulties
from which he cannot extricate himself without
their help, and to ruin the country if necessary,
rather than lose their place ; they need it to
oppress the people under the pretext of national
necessity ; to find places for their creatures ; to
rig the markets, and to establish in secret a thousand odious monopolies ; they need it to satisfy
their passions, and to get rid of each other ; and
they need it to get the prince into their power
by drawing him away from the Court when
dangerous intrigues are formed against them there.
They would lose all these resources by a Perpetual
Peace. And yet people never cease asking why,
if this project is possible, princes have not adopted
it. They do not see there is nothing impossible
in the project except that it should be adopted
by these men. What then will the ministers do
to oppose it ? What they have always done ;
they will turn it into ridicule.

We are not to assume with the Abbé de Saint-
Pierre, again, even given the goodwill that we
shall never find either in the prince or his
ministers, that it would be easy to find a favour-

l'exécution de ce systême ; car il faudroit pour cela que la somme des intérêts particuliers ne l'emportât pas sur l'intérêt commun, et que chacun crût voir dans le bien de tous le plus grand bien qu'il peut espérer pour lui-même. Or ceci demande un concours de sagesse dans tant de têtes et un concours de rapports dans tant d'intérêts, qu'on ne doit guère espérer du hasard l'accord fortuit de toutes les circonstances nécessaires : cependant si cet accord n'a pas lieu, il n'y a que la force qui puisse y suppléer ; et alors il n'est plus question de persuader, mais de contraindre, et il ne faut plus écrire des livres, mais lever des troupes.

Ainsi, quoique le projet fût très sage, les moyens de l'exécuter se sentoient de la simplicité de l'auteur. Il s'imaginoit bonnement qu'il ne falloit qu'assembler un congrès, y proposer ses articles, qu'on les alloit signer, et que tout seroit fait. Convenons que, dans tous les projets de cet honnête homme, il voyoit assez bien l'effet des choses quand elles seroient établies, mais il jugeoit comme un enfant des moyens de les établir.

Je ne voudrois, pour prouver que le projet de la république chrétienne n'est pas chimérique, que nommer son premier auteur : car assurément Henri IV n'étoit pas fou, ni Sully vision-

able moment to put this scheme into operation ; for it would be necessary for this, that the sum of private interests should not outweigh the common interest, and that everyone should believe himself to see in the good of all the greatest good he can hope for himself. Now this demands a concurrence of wisdom in so many heads and a fortuitous concurrence of so many interests, such as chance can hardly be expected to bring about. But in default of such an agreement the only thing left is force, and then it is no longer a question of persuading but of compelling, and instead of writing books you will have to raise troops.

Thus although the project was a very wise one, the means proposed for its execution betray the artlessness of its author. He supposed it was simply necessary to assemble a congress, propose his articles to it, have them signed and all would be settled. It must be admitted that, in all his projects, this worthy man saw clearly enough what their effect would be when they were once established, but that he judged like a child of the means for establishing them.

In order to prove that the project of the Christian republic is not a chimera, I wish merely to recall its first author; for assuredly Henry IV (12) was not a fool nor Sully (13) a

naire. L'abbé de Saint-Pierre s'autorisoit de ces grands noms pour renouveler leur systême. Mais quelle différence dans le temps, dans les circonstances, dans la proposition, dans la manière de la faire, et dans son auteur ! Pour en juger, jetons un coup-d'œil sur la situation générale des choses au moment choisi par Henri IV pour l'exécution de son projet.

La grandeur de Charles-Quint, qui régnoit sur une partie du monde et faisoit trembler l'autre, l'avoit fait aspirer à la monarchie universelle avec de grands moyens de succès et de grands talents pour les employer ; son fils, plus riche et moins puissant, suivant sans relâche un projet qu'il n'étoit pas capable d'exécuter, ne laissa pas de donner à l'Europe des inquiétudes continuelles ; et la maison d'Autriche avoit pris un tel ascendant sur les autres puissances, que nul prince ne régnoit en sûreté s'il n'étoit bien avec elle. Philippe III, moins habile encore que son père, hérita de toutes ses prétentions. L'effroi de la puissance espagnole tenoit encore l'Europe en respect, et l'Espagne continuoit à dominer plutôt par l'habitude de commander que par le pouvoir de se faire obéir. En effet, la révolte des Pays-Bas, les armements contre l'Angleterre, les guerres civiles de France, avoient épuisé les forces d'Espagne et les trésors des Indes ; la

visionary. The Abbé de Saint-Pierre used the authority of these great names to revive their scheme. But what a difference in the times, the circumstances, the proposition, in the manner of making it, and in its author! To judge of this, let us glance at the general situation at the moment chosen by Henry IV for the execution of his project.

The great power of Charles V, who reigned over one half of the world and made the other tremble, led him to aspire to universal monarchy. He had great resources to achieve success and great talents to employ them. His son, richer but less powerful, never abandoning a project which he was incapable of executing, was a constant cause of disquiet to Europe; and the house of Austria had obtained such an ascendancy over the other powers, that no prince reigned securely if he were not on good terms with it. Philip III, though even less able than his father, inherited all his high notions. Fear of the power of Spain still kept Europe in awe, and Spain continued to dominate, but more through the habit of command than by the power of making herself obeyed. In fact the revolt of the Netherlands, the Armada against England, and civil wars in France, had exhausted Spain's strength and the treasure of the Indies. The house of

maison d'Autriche, partagée en deux branches, n'agissoit plus avec le même concert ; et, quoique l'empereur s'efforçât de maintenir ou recouvrer en Allemagne l'autorité de Charles-Quint, il ne faisoit qu'aliéner les princes et fomenter des ligues qui ne tardèrent pas d'éclore et faillirent à le détrôner. Ainsi se préparoit de loin la décadence de la maison d'Autriche et le rétablissement de la liberté commune. Cependant nul n'osoit le premier hasarder de secouer le joug, et s'exposer seul à la guerre ; l'exemple de Henri IV même, qui s'en étoit tiré si mal, ôtoit le courage à tous les autres. D'ailleurs, si l'on excepte le duc de Savoie, trop foible et trop subjugué pour rien entreprendre, il n'y avoit pas, parmi tant de souverains, un seul homme de tête en état de former et soutenir une entreprise ; chacun attendoit du temps et des circonstances le moment de briser ses fers. Voilà quel étoit en gros l'état des choses quand Henri forma le plan de la république chrétienne et se prépara à l'exécuter. Projet bien grand, bien admirable en lui-même, et dont je ne veux pas ternir l'honneur, mais qui, ayant pour raison secrète l'espoir d'abaisser un ennemi redoutable, recevoit de ce pressant motif une activité qu'il eût difficilement tirée de la seule utilité commune.

Austria, divided into two branches, no longer acted with the same unity, and although the emperor strained every nerve to maintain or recover the authority of Charles V in Germany, he succeeded only in alienating the princes and fomenting leagues, which quickly came to a head and went near to dethroning him. Such were the slow stages which prepared the decay of the house of Austria, and the restoration of European liberty. Nevertheless no one dared to be the first to venture to shake off the yoke and to expose himself alone to the risks of war. The example of Henry IV, who himself came off so badly, had taken the heart out of all the others. Moreover, if one excepts the Duke of Savoy, too weak and cowed to undertake anything, there was not amongst so many sovereigns a single man of ability who was so situated as to form and carry through such an enterprise; each one was looking to time and circumstances for the moment to break his fetters. Such was roughly the state of things when Henry formed the plan of the Christian republic and prepared to carry it into execution. A very great project indeed and a very admirable one in itself; I have no wish to dim its glory. But, prompted as it was by the secret hope of humbling a formidable enemy, it acquired from that cogent motive a momentum

Voyons maintenant quels moyens ce grand homme avoit employés à préparer une si haute entreprise. Je compterois volontiers pour le premier d'en avoir bien vu toutes les difficultés ; de telle sorte qu'ayant formé ce projet dès son enfance, il le médita toute sa vie, et réserva l'exécution pour sa vieillesse : conduite qui prouve premièrement ce désir ardent et soutenu qui seul, dans les choses difficiles, peut vaincre les grands obstacles, et, de plus, cette sagesse patiente et réfléchie qui s'aplanit les routes de longue main à force de prévoyance et de préparation. Car il y a bien de la différence entre les entreprises necessaires dans lesquelles la prudence même veut qu'on donne quelque chose au hasard, et celles que le succès seul peut justifier, parcequ'ayant pu se passer de les faire on n'a dû les tenter qu'à coup sûr. Le profond secret qu'il garda toute sa vie, jusqu'au moment de l'exécution, étoit encore aussi essentiel que difficile dans une si grande affaire, où le concours de tant de gens étoit nécessaire, et que tant de gens avoient intérêt de traverser. Il paroît que, quoiqu'il eût mis la plus grande partie de l'Europe dans son parti et qu'il fût ligué avec les plus puissants potentats, il n'eut jamais qu'un seul confident qui connût toute l'étendue de son

which it could hardly have drawn from the incentive of the common good.

Now let us see what means this great man had employed for so high an enterprise. First and foremost I should be disposed to put the fact that he had foreseen all the difficulties of the task so that having formed this project in his youth, he pondered it all his life, and allotted its execution to his old age—a course of conduct which in the first place shows that ardent and sustained will which alone, in difficult matters, can overcome great obstacles, and smooth the path to success by far-sighted preparations. For there is a good deal of difference between necessary enterprises, in which prudence itself requires that something should be left to chance, and those that success alone can justify, because, there being no need to undertake them, they ought not to be attempted unless success is certain. The profound secrecy which he preserved throughout his life and up to the moment of execution was as essential as it was difficult in so great an enterprise, where the joint action of so many people was required, and when so many had an interest in thwarting it. It appears that although he had the greater part of Europe on his side and was in league with the most powerful potentates, he had but one confidant who knew

plan, et, par un bonheur que le ciel n'accorda qu'au meilleur des rois, ce confident fut un ministre intègre. Mais sans que rien transpirât de ses grands desseins, tout marchoit en silence vers leur exécution. Deux fois Sully étoit allé à Londres ; la partie étoit liée avec le roi Jacques, et le roi de Suède étoit engagé de son côté : la ligue étoit conclue avec les protestants d'Allemagne ; on étoit même sûr des princes d'Italie, et tous concouroient au grand but sans pouvoir dire quel il étoit, comme les ouvriers qui travaillent séparément aux pièces d'une nouvelle machine dont ils ignorent la forme et l'usage. Qu'est-ce donc qui favorisoit ce mouvement général ? Etoit-ce la paix perpétuelle que nul ne prévoyoit, et dont peu se seroient souciés ? étoit-ce l'intérêt public, qui n'est jamais celui de personne ? L'abbé de Saint-Pierre eût pu l'espérer. Mais réellement chacun ne travailloit que dans la vue de son intérêt particulier, que Henri avoit eu le secret de leur montrer à tous sous une face très attrayante. Le roi d'Angleterre avoit à se délivrer des continuelles conspirations des catholiques de son royaume, toutes fomentées par l'Espagne. Il trouvoit de plus un grand

the whole compass of his plan, and by such a
stroke of good fortune as heaven grants only to
the best of kings, this confidant was an upright
minister. Everything moved silently towards
completion without any of his great designs
becoming known. Twice Sully had been to
London; a compact had been made with King
James I. The King of Sweden had pledged
himself for his part, a league had been made with
the Protestants of Germany; and even the
Italian princes had been secured. All were
contributing to the great end without being
able to say what it was, like workmen who work
separately on the parts of a new machine of whose
appearance and use they are ignorant. What was
it then that was furthering this general movement? Was it the Perpetual Peace that no one
foresaw, and about which few would have cared?
Was it the public interest, which is never the
interest of anyone in particular? The Abbé
de Saint-Pierre might have hoped so. But in
reality they were all working only from the point
of view of their own private interests, which
Henry had the secret of presenting to each of
them under a very attractive guise. The King
of England had to be rescued from the perpetual
conspiracies formed by his own Catholic subjects,
all of which were fomented by Spain. He also

121

avantage a l'affranchissement des Provinces-Unies, qui lui coûtoient beaucoup a soutenir, et le mettoient chaque jour à la veille d'une guerre qu'il redoutoit, ou à laquelle il aimoit mieux contribuer une fois avec tous les autres, afin de s'en delivrer pour toujours. Le roi de Suède vouloit s'assurer de la Poméranie et mettre un pied dans l'Allemagne. L'électeur palatin, alors protestant et chef de la confession d'Augsbourg, avoit des vues sur la Bohême et entroit dans toutes celles du roi d'Angleterre. Les princes d'Allemagne avoient à réprimer les usurpations de la maison d'Autriche. Le duc de Savoie obtenoit Milan et la couronne de Lombardie qu'il désiroit avec ardeur. Le pape même, fatigué de la tyrannie espagnole, étoit de la partie au moyen du royaume de Naples qu'on lui avoit promis. Les Hollandois, mieux payés que tous les autres, gagnoient l'assurance de leur liberté. Enfin, outre l'intérêt commun d'abaisser une puissance orgueilleuse qui vouloit dominer partout, chacun en avoit un particulier, très vif, tres sensible, et qui n'étoit point balancé par la crainte de substituer un tyran à l'autre, puisqu'il étoit convenu que les conquêtes seroient par-

looked to reap some advantage from the liberation of the United Provinces, for they had cost him a good deal to sustain, and brought him every day to the eve of a war which he dreaded, or to put it another way, one in which he preferred to take his share once for all with the rest, so that he might be quit of it for ever.

The King of Sweden wished to secure Pomerania and to get a footing in Germany. The Elector Palatine, then a Protestant and the head of the Augsburg Confession, had his eye on Bohemia, and shared all the hopes of the King of England. The princes of Germany had to repress the usurpations of the house of Austria. The Duke of Savoy was to obtain Milan and the Crown of Lombardy which he passionately coveted. The Pope himself, weary of the Spanish tyranny, belonged to the Coalition because the Kingdom of Naples had been promised to him as a consideration. The Dutch, better paid than all the rest, gained security for their liberty.

In a word, besides their common interest each of them had a special, personal and very lively interest in humiliating a proud power which wanted to dominate them all. This was not outweighed by the fear of substituting one tyrant for another, since it was agreed that conquests were to be shared alike between all the Allies,

tagées entre tous les alliés, excepté la France et
l'Angleterre qui ne pouvoient rien garder pour
elles. C'en étoit assez pour calmer les plus inquiets
sur l'ambition de Henri IV. Mais ce sage prince
n'ignoroit pas qu'en ne se réservant rien par ce
traité, il y gagnoit pourtant plus qu'aucun autre ;
car, sans rien ajouter à son patrimoine, il lui
suffisoit de diviser celui du seul plus puissant
que lui, pour devenir le plus puissant lui-même ;
et l'on voit très clairement qu'en prenant toutes
les précautions qui pouvoient assurer le succès
de l'entreprise, il ne négligeoit pas celles qui
devoient lui donner la primauté dans le corps
qu'il vouloit instituer.

De plus, ses apprêts ne se bornoient point à
former au-dehors des ligues redoutables, ni à
contracter alliance avec ses voisins et ceux de
son ennemi. En intéressant tant de peuples à
l'abaissement du premier potentat de l'Europe,
il n'oublioit pas de se mettre en état par lui-
même de le devenir à son tour. Il employa
quinze ans de paix à faire des préparatifs dignes
de l'entreprise qu'il méditoit. Il remplit d'argent
ses coffres, ses arsenaux d'artillerie, d'armes, de
munitions ; il ménagea de loin des ressources

except France and England, who would not be able to keep anything for themselves. That was enough to calm the most suspicious mind on the score of Henry's ambition. But that wise prince was well aware that, in spite of reserving nothing for himself by this treaty, he none the less stood to gain more from it than any of the others. Without adding anything to his patrimony, it was enough for him to divide that of the only ruler more powerful than he, in order to become the most powerful one himself; and it can be seen very clearly that while taking all the precautions which could assure the success of the enterprise, he did not neglect those which were to give him the supremacy in the confederation he wished to create.

Moreover, his preparations were not limited to making formidable leagues abroad nor to contracting alliances with his neighbours and his enemies' neighbours. While engaging so many people in the downfall of the first potentate of Europe, he did not forget to provide on his own account for getting hold of the same position. He spent fifteen years of peace in making preparations worthy of the enterprise he meditated. He filled his coffers with money and his arsenals with artillery, arms, and munitions. He economised his resources for a long time beforehand against

pour les besoins imprévus : mais il fit plus que tout cela sans doute en gouvernant sagement ses peuples, en déracinant insensiblement toutes les semences de divisions, et en mettant un si bon ordre à ses finances, qu'elles pussent fournir à tout sans fouler ses sujets ; de sorte que, tranquille au-dedans et redoutable au-dehors, il se vit en état d'armer et d'entretenir soixante mille hommes et vingt vaisseaux de guerre, de quitter son royaume sans y laisser la moindre source de désordre, et de faire la guerre durant six ans sans toucher à ses revenus ordinaires ni mettre un sou de nouvelles impositions.

A tant de préparatifs, ajoutez, pour la conduite de l'entreprise, le même zèle et la même prudence qui l'avoient formée, tant de la part de son ministre que de la sienne ; enfin, à la tête des expéditions militaires, un capitaine tel que lui, tandis que son adversaire n'en avoit plus à lui opposer : et vous jugerez si rien de ce qui peut annoncer un heureux succès manquoit à l'espoir du sien. Sans avoir pénétré ses vues, l'Europe attentive à ses immenses préparatifs en attendoit l'effet avec une sorte de frayeur. Un léger prétexte alloit commencer cette grande révolu-

unforeseen needs ; but he did even a great deal more, surely, by governing his people wisely, by uprooting by imperceptible degrees all the seeds of discord, and by putting his finances into such good order that he was able to provide for everything without oppressing his subjects. So that in tranquillity at home and formidable abroad, he was able to arm and maintain 60,000 troops and 20 men-o'-war ; he could absent himself from his kingdom without leaving behind him the least germ of disorder there ; and make war for six years without touching his ordinary revenues or putting an extra penny on taxation.

To all these preparations must be added an assurance that the enterprise would be conducted with the same zeal and prudence which had initiated it, both on his minister's part and his own ; and finally that there would be a captain equal to himself at the head of the military operations, whilst his adversary had no competent commander to set against him ; and you can judge whether anything that might augur a hopeful issue was lacking to his cause. Unable to fathom his intentions, the whole of Europe watched these immense preparations, and waited in awe for their outcome. Some light pretext was on the point of starting this gigantic revolution, and a war, which was to have been the end of war, was

tion ; une guerre, qui devoit être la dernière, préparoit une paix immortelle, quand un événement dont l'horrible mystère doit augmenter l'effroi vint bannir à jamais le dernier espoir du monde. Le même coup qui trancha les jours de ce bon roi replongea l'Europe dans d'éternelles guerres qu'elle ne doit plus espérer de voir finir. Quoi qu'il en soit, voilà les moyens que Henri IV avoit rassemblés pour former le même établissement que l'abbé de Saint-Pierre prétendoit faire avec un livre.

Qu'on ne dise donc point que si son systême n'a pas été adopté, c'est qu'il n'étoit pas bon : qu'on dise au contraire qu'il étoit trop bon pour être adopté ; car le mal et les abus, dont tant de gens profitent, s'introduisent d'eux-mêmes. Mais ce qui est utile au public ne s'introduit guère que par la force, attendu que les intérêts particuliers y sont presque toujours opposés. Sans doute la paix perpétuelle est à présent un projet bien absurde ; mais qu'on nous rende un Henri IV et un Sully, la paix perpétuelle redeviendra un projet raisonnable : ou plutôt admirons un si beau plan, mais consolons-nous de ne pas le voir exécuter ; car cela ne peut se faire que par des moyens violents et redoutables à l'humanité.

about to usher in eternal peace, when an event, whose dreadful mystery can only increase its horror, came to banish for ever the world's last hope. The same blow which cut short the days of this good king, plunged Europe again into everlasting wars, of which it can no longer hope to see the end.

Let that be as it may, those were the means Henry IV had prepared for the foundation of the same institution that the Abbé de Saint-Pierre expected to establish with a book.

Let no one say then if his system has not been adopted that it was not a good one ; let us say on the contrary that it was too good to be adopted, for the wrongs and the abuses out of which so many people profit come about of themselves. But what is of benefit to the public is scarcely ever brought about except by force, seeing that private interests are almost always opposed to it. Without doubt Perpetual Peace is at present an absurd dream ; but when another Henry IV and Sully appear, Perpetual Peace will come back again as a reasonable project ; or rather, while we admire so fair a scheme, let us console ourselves for the fact that it was not carried into execution, by the reflection that it could only have been done by violent means which would have staggered humanity.

On ne voit point de ligues fédératives s'établir autrement que par des révolutions : et, sur ce principe, qui de nous oseroit dire si cette ligue européenne est à désirer ou à craindre ? Elle feroit peut-être plus de mal tout d'un coup qu'elle n'en préviendroit pour des siècles.

There is no prospect of federative leagues being established otherwise than by revolutions, and on this assumption which of us would venture to say whether this European League is more to be desired or feared ?   It might perhaps do more harm all of a sudden than it could prevent for centuries.

NOTES

NOTE 1 (p. xxv). Jean François de Bastide (1724–1798) was a busy man of letters whose comedies and other ephemeral works attracted the sarcasm of Voltaire.

NOTE 2 (p. xxv). Charles-Irénée Castel, Abbé de Saint-Pierre (1658–1743), was the author of the treatise which Rousseau edited. As an old man he associated with the young Rousseau at Chenonceaux, and considerably impressed him. The Count was his nephew.

NOTE 3 (p. xxv). The *Polysynodie*, published in 1718, was the other work by the Abbé which Rousseau edited. It was a scheme for decentralising the monarchy of Louis XIV.

NOTE 4 (p. 7). Rousseau means, of course, that the half-way stage between a state of nature and a unified world-government has led to wars between nations even worse than the duels and private wars which national governments had suppressed.

NOTE 5 (p. 9). Amphictyonic Leagues existed in Greece from time immemorial. They were associations of neighbouring tribes or cities, made by Hellenes for the purpose of mutual intercourse and for the protection of a common temple or sanctuary. There were many such leagues of which the Delphic was the most important. The members registered a vow as recorded by Æchines

(*The False Legation*, ii, 115) : " We will not destroy any city of the Amphictyons, nor cut off the supply of running water, either in war or peace, and if any member break this oath, we will make war upon him and destroy his cities, and if any member plunder the property of the god, or be privy to any such design, or make any plan to that effect, we will punish him with hand and foot and voice and all our power. A terrible curse was affixed to the oath."

It will be seen that the germ of such organisations as the League of Nations is to be found in the Amphictyonic Leagues.

The Lucumo was a leader, apparently of a priestly character, among the Etruscans. Each city had a Lucumo and the power of the King, who was elected for life, was inferior to that of the Lucumo. Livy (iv. 23) mentions an Etrurian League. He records that the Veii and Falisci, two members of the League, sent envoys to all the twelve cities, asking them to convene a conference of the whole of Etruria at the Temple of Voltumna.

Rousseau seems to have confused the Lucumones (leaders) with the *Concilium.*

See Macaulay, *Horatius* :

> " And plainly and more plainly
>   Now might the burghers know,
> By port and vest, by horse and crest,
>   Each warlike Lucumo."

The Latin League existed from very early times, under the traditional leadership of Alba, the most ancient

133

of the Latin cantons. There were thirty cities in the League. Mommsen (i. 50) : " The rendezvous of this union was . . . the ' Latin festival ' (*feriæ Latinæ*), at which, on the ' Mount of Alba,' (*Mons Albanus, Monte Cavo*), upon a day annually appointed by the chief magistrate for the purpose, an ox was offered in sacrifice by the assembled Latin stock to the ' Latin God ' (*Jupiter Latinaris*)." The Latin League, however, seems to have been almost entirely a military league, without exercising any humanising influence, such as those practised by the Amphictyonic.

See again Macaulay, *The Battle of Lake Regillus* :

> " How the Lake Regillus
> Bubbled with crimson foam,
> What time the Thirty Cities
> Came forth to war on Rome."

In fact, the Gauls had not much federal organisation, although they made attempts to league their cantons together when attacked by Cæsar. This want of unity led to their rapid conquest. As Tacitus says in the *Agricola*—" While the individual groups fight, the whole are conquered "—(*Dum singuli pugnant, universi vincuntur*).

The Achæan League is here correctly described by Rousseau. " Early in the third century B.C., the League struggled unsuccessfully against Antigonus Gonatas." Grote says (x. 326, 7) : " The Achæan league . . . developed itself afterwards as a renovated sprout from the ruined tree of Grecian liberty, though never attaining to

anything better than a feeble and puny life, nor capable of sustaining itself without foreign aid."

As regards the German, Swiss, and French Assemblies, they are so closely interwoven with the national life that a study of their history is equivalent to a study of the history of the respective countries.

NOTE 6 (p. 11). The Emperor Claudius, in a speech which has been preserved, brought forward a motion in the Senate for admitting Gaulish chiefs to senatorial rank.

NOTE 7 (p. 13). Theodosius II (*d.* 450 A.D.) was less celebrated than his grandfather, Theodosius the Great. But he is memorable for having published the Codex Theodosianus in 438, which is a collection of imperial contributions to guide the action of public officials. This is one of our main sources of information about the government of the Empire in the fifth century.

Justinian's memorable *Corpus Juris* was given the effect of law in 534 A.D. Gibbon says (*Decline c.* xliv.) : " The vain titles of the victories of Justinian are crumbled into dust ; but the name of the legislator is inscribed on a fair and everlasting monument. Under his reign, and by his care, the civil jurisprudence was digested in the immortal works of the *Code,* the *Pandects,* and the *Institutes* ; the public reason of the Romans has been silently or studiously transfused into the domestic institutions of Europe ; and the laws of Justinian still command the respect or obedience of independent nations."

NOTE 8 (p. 17). Bartholus (1314–1357) was one of the most esteemed of Italian civil jurists. He lectured at

135

Perugia which he raised to great eminence among law schools. He won much fame by his *Commentaries on the Code of Justinian.*

NOTE 9 (p. 37). According to the Mercantilist theory the only true form of wealth was gold and silver, and the object of commerce was to export goods and import the precious metals.

NOTE 10 (p. 37). This date, 1756, is significant. At that time England was starting on the Seven Years' War under the incompetent guidance of the Duke of Newcastle, and disasters came thick and fast. The depression was aggravated the next year by the publication of Dr. John Brown's *Estimate*, to which Burke refers in his *Regicide Peace*. The *Estimate*, which sought to prove " that a frivolous effeminacy was become the national character," acquired great popularity and many people formed the opinion that the nation was old and decrepit and destined shortly to perish in the natural course of things. Burke, in his opening pages, gives a masterly refutation of this fallacy and the pessimism, as applied to 1757 and all other times, remarking, with one of those flashes of penetrative reason that have made his great reputation, that " commonwealths are not physical but moral essences." As it happened, before Rousseau penned this note in 1761, England had won " all her glory," defeating France by sea and in Canada and in India, and thus founding two great Dominions.

NOTE 11 (p. 71). " The resignation of all the eastern conquests of Trajan was the first measure of his reign. He restored to the Parthians the election of an indepen-

dent sovereign ; withdrew the Roman garrisons from the provinces of Armenia, Mesopotamia, and Assyria ; and in compliance with the precepts of Augustus, once more established the Euphrates as the frontier of the empire." Gibbon, c. 1.

NOTE 12 (p. 113). Henry IV (1553–1610), the ablest and best of French kings. After long wars he succeeded in consolidating France and composing the religious troubles by obtaining toleration for the Huguenots.

NOTE 13 (p. 113). Maximilien de Béthune, Duc de Sully (1560–1641), was the ablest minister of Henry IV. It was he who advised the King to become a Roman Catholic. According to his own account he at first regarded the scheme of a perpetual peace as visionary, but he was at last converted to Henry's view. Soon after his master's assassination he retired into private life and wrote the famous Memoirs which are our sole authority for the scheme.

INDEX

INDEX

S

Saint-Pierre, v–xiv; xix; xxii; xxiv; xxv; 64, 65; 96–9; 110, 111; 114, 115; 120, 121; 128, 129; 132

Sardinia, 52, 53

Savoy, Duke of, 116, 117

Soviet, xviii

Spain, 52, 53; 114, 115; 122, 123

Sully, ix; x; 112, 113; 120, 121; 128, 129

Sweden, 120–3

Swiss League, ix

T

Tacitus, 134

Tartars, 80, 81

Theodosian Code, 12, 13

Theodosius II, 135

Theodosius the Great, 135

Touraine, 84, 85

Trajan, 137

Turkey, xvii

Turks, 40, 41; 80, 81

U

Utilitarian, vi

Utrecht, Peace of, viii

V

Varignon, vi

Vaughan, xxiii

Veii, 133

Venezuela, xiii

Venice, 132

Voltumna, 133

W

Westphalia, Treaty of, 34, 35

141

BENTHAM
PLAN FOR AN UNIVERSAL AND PERPETUAL PEACE

BY JEREMY BENTHAM

1786—1789

PEACE
CLASSICS
VOL.
VI

WITH AN INTRODUCTION

BY

C. JOHN COLOMBOS, LL.D.

Of University College and the London School of Economics,
and of the Middle Temple, Barrister-at-Law

PEACE BOOK COMPANY
5 Goodwin's Court, St. Martin's Lane,
London, W.C.2

Originally Published by the Grotius Society
Re-issued by the Peace Book Company
1939
General Editor, David Ogg, M.A.

(iii .)

CONTENTS.

INTRODUCTION.

No series of legal historical classics for students of the Science of Law would be complete without the inclusion of Jeremy Bentham among its representative authors, and his *Plea for an Universal and Perpetual Peace* is peculiarly appropriate as an example of the ideas of a great thinker at a time (1786-1789) when a great political upheaval in France had excited the hopes of philosophic idealists and provoked intenseness of feeling and general criticism of existing institutions and conventional modes of thought. A comparison of his main suggestion in this treatise with our present attitude of mind towards international relations, and the realisation in general practice of such lofty ideals as those set forth in the Covenant of the League of Nations, shows how far the civilised world to-day has moved towards general peace—the unity between the nations which has been thought of as merely visionary. Bentham is the philosophical lawyer of his age, with vision and clear reasoning and practical common sense; and he has had more effect on our own law than any other man in the way of reform and enlightenment.

The span of his life, eighty-five years, extended from the middle of the eighteenth century well into the nineteenth. He saw the rise of the United States, the European convulsion of the Seven Years' War, the attempted realisation of the theories of philosophic thinkers and authors, and finally the revolt of the populations of the chief European States against the reactionary power and spirit of Governments inspired by dynastic aims and crazy of imperial aggrandisement. Our own country was first beginning its era of peaceful reform by political emancipation, and Bentham thus forms a connecting link between two widely-differing periods of thought and action.

The main facts of his life may be briefly stated; they are to be found in detail in the *Dictionary of National Biography* and other well-known works of reference. Born at Houndsditch on February 15, 1747 (8), the son and grandson of lawyers, he was educated at Westminster School (1755-1760) and Queen's

College, Oxford (1760-1763), and took his Bachelor of Arts
1763, and his Master of Arts 1766, and left Oxford 1767.
Meantime he had entered as a student at Lincoln's Inn (1763),
of which he became a Master of the Bench in 1817.

Bentham, however, made no attempt to succeed in his
profession. His mind was entirely set upon the task of social
reform. Even from early student days his imagination was
filled with a comprehensive notion of the public good. When
hardly twenty-two he had read in Priestley of the greatest
happiness of the greatest number, an idea which he at once
appropriated and wrought into the very texture of his works.
In his own words, public good had no limits other than those
of the habitable globe. This explains why Bentham invariably
took as a basis for his reforms " the common and equal utility
of all nations." To be judged fairly, in fact, Bentham must
be judged as a citizen of the world, imbued with a most ardent
love for humanity. The system upon which he proceeded was
to inquire of all institutions whether their existence was justified
by their utility. If not, his efforts would tend in suggesting a
new form of institution which would answer the desired purpose
of the greatest happiness of mankind. In an introduction to
his works written in 1837, Burton gives a long list of reforms
first advanced by Bentham and subsequently adopted by the
British Legislature. Any review, however, of the salutary
influence exercised by Bentham would be sadly incomplete if
it were confined to his own country. His works embraced the
whole of the civilised world, and the constitutions and practically
all of the laws of the new States which sprung up during his
time show deep tracings of his teachings. His writings have
been, and remain, " a storehouse of instruction for statesmen,
an armoury for legal reformers." " Pillé par tout le monde,"
as Talleyrand said of him, " il est toujours riche."

Bentham died on June 6, 1832, and left his body to be dissected
for the benefit of mankind. His skeleton, clothed in his usual
clothes, is kept in University College, London.

Much of his work remains unpublished, although a great part
of his MSS., which fill eighty wooden boxes, as much deserves
publication as that which has already appeared in the Press. His
published writings cover the whole sphere of ethics, logic, and

political science. Bentham's principal contribution, however, was in the field of jurisprudence. In the light of his teachings, law gained a new dignity, and became " the science which held in its hand the happiness of men and nations."

On the special subject of International Law, Bentham's work is contained within a comparatively small compass. His *Principles of International Law* hardly cover twenty-four pages out of the eleven thickly-printed volumes of the collected works published in 1838 by John Bowring. But within this narrow limit are comprised reforms which appear primordial at the present time, such as disarmament, the institution of an International Court, and the burning question of the publicity of foreign negotiations and treaties. It is not unimportant to remark, on the other hand, that it was Bentham who first coined the words "International Law" in order to establish a distinction between the mutual transactions of Sovereigns as such and laws calculated for internal government, a distinction which had never been definitely made in any previous work on the subject. The first serious impulse to the codification of International Law was also initiated by Bentham, who seems to have forestalled, in a great measure, the modern movement towards a general code of the main rules of that law.

Bentham's *Principles of International Law* are collected from MSS. which bear date 1786 to 1789 and comprise four essays :—

(1) Objects of International Law.
(2) Subjects, or the Personal Extent of the Dominion of the Laws.
(3) War, considered in respect of its Causes and Consequences.
(4) A Plan for an Universal and Perpetual Peace.

This last, the longest and most important of the four essays, is reprinted in full here. A short commentary, however, of the three other essays may perhaps be also usefully made at this stage, since all the four essays are closely related to each other.

FIRST ESSAY.—OBJECTS OF INTERNATIONAL LAW.

Bentham describes the objects of International Law for any given nation as being :—

(1) Utility general. in so far as it consists in doing no injury

to the other nations, saving the regard which is proper
to its own well-being;

(2) Utility general, in so far as it consists in doing the greatest
good possible to other nations;

(3) Utility general, in so far as it consists in the given nation
not receiving any injury from other nations respectively;

(4) Utility general, in so far as it consists in receiving the
greatest possible benefit from all other nations, saving
always the regard due to the well-being of these
nations;

(5) In case of war, make such arrangements that the least
possible evil may be produced, consistently with the
acquisition of the good which is sought for.

Expressed in the most general manner, the task which a
legislator preparing an international code would propose to
himself as his object would, therefore, in Bentham's opinion,
be the greatest happiness of all nations taken together.

Bentham was opposed to war, which he considered not only
as an evil, but as the complication of all other evils. Still, he
believed that there might possibly be circumstances justifying
war when no other method of obtaining satisfaction by an
injured complainant could be found, and where there was no
arbitrator between the conflicting nations sufficiently strong to
take from them all hope of resistance. When the worst
happened, and hostilities broke out, Bentham advocated an
appeal to the tribunal of public opinion for the purpose of
controlling the conduct of war and preventing unnecessary evils
and the consequent infringement of the greatest happiness
principle.

Second Essay.—Subjects, or the Personal Extent of the Dominion of the Laws.

In this essay Bentham lays down the main rules which ought
to govern the allegiance of a person to a given State. Proceeding
as usual on the exhaustive plan, he examines the grounds upon
which a Sovereign can establish a claim of standing dominion
over his supposed subjects. Territorial dominion, although possessing most of the desired qualifications, is not a circumstance

of sufficient permanence, since the same individual who finds himself one day on land belonging to a given Sovereign may the next day transfer himself to the territory of another Sovereign. It would, therefore, be unwise to base the determining criterion on a situation which is liable to change at any time.

To Bentham's mind, the test ought to rest on *an event*. Such an event is that afforded by *birth*, which must necessarily happen for a man to exist, and which cannot happen a second time. But if birth be the ground of dominion, it is only in virtue of the presumption which it affords of the other concurrent circumstance of presence or residence. It is true that in almost every State there are some who emigrate from the dominion within which they were born. But in almost every State it is otherwise with by far the greatest number. In civilised nations the greater part of mankind are *glebæ ascriptitii*—inhabitants of the soil on which they were born.

It is in this way that the dominion over the soil confers a *de facto* dominion over the greater part of the natives, its inhabitants, and that they are treated as owing a permanent allegiance to the Sovereign of that soil; and, speaking generally, there seemed to Bentham no reason why, judging upon the principle of utility, it should not be deemed to be so even *de jure*.

THIRD ESSAY.—WAR, CONSIDERED IN RESPECT OF ITS CAUSES AND CONSEQUENCES.

When a State has received what it considers as an injury from another State, there being no supreme controlling authority between nations, it must either submit to the injury, induce the other State to consent to the appointment of a common Judge, or else go to war. This affords Bentham the occasion for setting out an enumeration of the principal causes or occasions of war, which, according to his classification, may be grouped into two big categories:—(1) Offences, real or pretended, of the citizens of one State towards the citizens of another State caused by the interests of the citizens; and (2) offences, real or pretended, of the citizens of one State

towards the citizens of another State caused by the interests or pretensions of Sovereigns.

As to wars, they may be either (i) *bona fide*, and the remedy against these is to be found in the establishment of the Tribunal of Peace, which Bentham describes in his fourth essay; (ii) or wars of passion, and the remedy against these is to be found in reasoning, showing the repugnancy between passion, on the one hand, and justice, as well as interest, on the other; (iii) or lastly, wars of ambition, insolence, or rapine, and the remedy against these is again reasoning, showing the repugnancy between ambition and true interest.

In all these cases the utility of the State which thought itself aggrieved depended partly on its relative force, partly upon what appeared to have been the motive from which the injury originated. Where the aggressor was not actuated by any *mala fides*, it could never be for the advantage of the aggrieved State to go to war. If *mala fides* existed, whether even then it was worth while to have recourse to war depended on circumstances. If the injury was but a prelude to others, and proceeded from a disposition which only entire destruction could satisfy and war presented any tolerable chance of success, prudence and reason might join with passion in prescribing war as the only remedy in so desperate a disease. If, on the other hand, the aggression, though too flagrant not to be accompanied by *mala fides*, had for its origin some limited object, the attainment of which would prevent war, then it might be infinitely more prudent to submit to it rather than encounter the calamities of war.

When war had broken out, a palliative for its evils could be found in the appointment of war residents to provide for prisoners, prevent violations of the laws of warfare, and act as a channel of communication between the belligerents, should an accommodation be desired.

FOURTH ESSAY.—A PLAN FOR AN UNIVERSAL AND PERPETUAL PEACE.

These remedies for suppressing the causes of war between States appeared to Bentham himself so inadequate that he suggested in his fourth essay an important plan for the main-

tenance of peace amongst nations. He based his plan upon two fundamental principles, both of which he considered essential to its success:—

(1) The reduction and fixation of the forces of the several States which composed the European Concert, or, in other words, disarmament.

(2) The emancipation of the colonial dependencies of each State. This emancipation was in harmony with Bentham's deep conviction that colonies, besides being a source of constant conflicts between nations, were of little or no utility to their mother country.

For the realisation of the first principle—that of world disarmament—Bentham advocated the conclusion of general and perpetual treaties limiting the number of naval and military forces to be kept by each State. In a stirring appeal to his countrymen, Bentham showed how such an agreement would have nothing in it which would be dishonourable or detrimental to the national dignity or pride of a State, but that, on the contrary, the nation which would get the start of the other in making the proposal would " crown itself with everlasting honour."

As a natural corollary to the maintenance of peace, Bentham urged the establishment of an International Court of Judicature for the determination of disputes between the several States. It is significant that the author, in his plea for an International Tribunal, was clearly of opinion that such a tribunal should not " be armed with any coercive powers," a reasoning which aptly applies to the present Permanent Court of International Justice.

Besides a Common Judicature, Bentham was also in favour of a Common Legislature between States. The proceedings of such a Congress or Diet, as Bentham styles it, were to be all public, and its functions were to consist (a) in recording its resolutions on all matters affecting the relations between the States composing it; (b) in causing those resolutions to be circulated among all the members; and (c) in placing under the ban of Europe any State which, after the lapse of a reasonable time, would refuse to conform itself to the Congress's decrees.

In Bentham's view, however, the most powerful instrument for the sanction of the Congress's resolutions was public opinion,

aided and encouraged by the liberty of the Press and the widest and most extensive circulation of the Congress's work.

Here, again, Bentham may be appropriately described as a pioneer of the present League of Nations, and his plan therefore deserves the closest study.

On another point—that of the secrecy of foreign negotiations— Bentham was also a forerunner of the modern demand for greater publicity. Taking as illustration of his arguments the Foreign Department of the British Cabinet of his time, he attempted to show that the principle of mystery surrounding the conclusion of International Treaties was not only altogether useless, but equally repugnant to the interests of liberty and peace. History proved, in fact, that it was the veil of secrecy cast over foreign negotiations that made it possible for Ministers in the past to plunge the nation into a war against its will. But if, as the author vigorously advocated in his writings, war is useless and of no profit to the interests of a State, or of advantage to the trade of its citizens, anything tending to minimise wars and preserve peace ought to be strenuously supported.

Bentham's conclusion on the whole question was that, as an inquiry into the facts governing international relations would abundantly prove, there was nowhere a real conflict between the interests of nations; but that, on the contrary, when States began to get better accustomed to public negotiations and to the performance of mutual services and obligations towards each other, they would daily find more inducements to preserve the blessings of peace and fewer causes to resort to war.

BIBLIOGRAPHY.

Bentham's *Works*, together with selections from his correspondence, a biography, and an introduction by J. H. Burton, were published by Dr. John Bowring in eleven volumes, Edinburgh, 1838-43.

Translations of Bentham's works have also appeared in most European languages, among which may be cited the French edition, *Œuvres*, prepared by P. E. L. Dumont and published in three volumes, Brussels, 1829-30, and the Spanish edition, *Coleccion de obras del celebre Jeremias Bentham*, prepared by B. Anduaga Espinosa and published in fourteen volumes, Madrid, 1841-43.

ATKINSON, C. M. *Jeremy Bentham, His Life and Works.* London. 1905.

COCK, HERMAN G. DE. *Jeremy Bentham, Proefschrift.* Utrecht. 1895.

DICEY, A. V. *Law and Opinion in England.* London. 1905. (pp. 125-209.)

EMPSON, Professor. " Jeremy Bentham," *Edinburgh Review.* Vol. 78. 1843. (pp. 460-516.)

HOLLAND, Sir THOMAS E. " Jeremy Bentham," *Encyclopædia Britannica.* Eleventh edition. Vol. III. (pp. 747-749.)

MACCUNN, JOHN. *Six Radical Thinkers.* London. 1910. (pp. 1-35.)

MACDONELL, Sir JOHN. " Jeremy Bentham," *Dictionary of National Biography.* Vol. IV. (pp. 268-280.)

MILL, JOHN STUART. *Early Essays.* (Three Essays on Bentham.) London. 1897.

MOHL, R. VON. *Geschichte und Literatur der Staatswissenschaften.* Vol. III. (pp. 595-635.)

NYS, ERNEST. *Etudes de droit international et de droit politique.* Brussels. 1901. (pp. 291-333.)

———— *Les Bentham Papers du British Museum.* Brussels. 1891.

SIEGWART, A. *Bentham's Werke und ihre Publikation.* Berlin. 1910.

WALLAS, GRAHAM. *Jeremy Bentham.* London. 1922.

WHEATON, H. *History of the Law of Nations.* New York. 1845. (pp. 328—44.)

WHITTAKER, T. *Report on Bentham's MSS.* London. 1892.

ZANE MAXCY, J. " Jeremy Bentham," *Great Jurists of the World.* London. 1913. (pp. 532—43.)

A PLAN FOR AN UNIVERSAL AND PERPETUAL PEACE.

The object of the present essay is to submit to the world a plan for an universal and perpetual peace. The globe is the field of dominion to which the author aspires; the Press the engine, and the only one he employs; the cabinet of mankind the theatre of his intrigue.

The happiest of mankind are sufferers by war; and the wisest, nay, even the least wise, are wise enough to ascribe the chief of their sufferings to that cause.

The following plan has for its basis two fundamental propositions:—(1) The reduction and fixation of the force of the several nations that compose the European system; and (2) the emancipation of the distant dependencies of each State (a). Each of these propositions has its distinct advantages, but neither of them, it will appear, would completely answer the purpose without the other.

As to the utility of such an universal and lasting peace, supposing a plan for that purpose practicable and likely to be adopted, there can be but one voice. The objection, and the only objection, to it is the apparent impracticability of it— that it is not only hopeless, but that to such a degree that any proposal to that effect deserves the name of visionary and ridiculous. This objection I shall endeavour, in the first place, to remove, for the removal of this prejudice may be necessary to procure for the plan a hearing.

What can be better suited to the preparing of men's minds for the reception of such a proposal than the proposal itself?

Let it not be objected that the age is not ripe for such a proposal. The more it wants of being ripe the sooner we should

(a) Two original writers have gone before me in this line, Dean Tucker and Dr. Anderson. The object of the first was to persuade the world of the inutility of war, but more particularly of the war then raging when he wrote; the object of the second to show the inutility of the colonies.

begin to do what can be done to ripen it; the more we should do to ripen it. A proposal of this sort is one of those things that can never come too early nor too late.

Who that bears the name of Christian can refuse the assistance of his prayers? What pulpit can forbear to second me with its eloquence? Catholics and Protestants, Church of England men and Dissenters, may all agree in this if in nothing else. I call upon them all to aid me with their countenance and their support.

The ensuing sheets are dedicated to the common welfare of all civilised nations, but more particularly of Great Britain and France.

The end in view is to recommend three grand objects— simplicity of government, national frugality, and peace.

Reflection has satisfied me of the truth of the following propositions :—

I. That it is not the interest of Great Britain to have any foreign dependencies whatsoever.

II. That it is not the interest of Great Britain to have any treaty of alliance, offensive or defensive, with any other Power whatsoever.

III. That it is not the interest of Great Britain to have any treaty with any Power whatsoever, for the purpose of possessing any advantage whatsoever in point of trade, to the exclusion of any other nation whatsoever.

IV. That it is not the interest of Great Britain to keep up any naval force beyond what may be sufficient to defend its commerce against pirates.

V. That it is not the interest of Great Britain to keep on foot any regulations whatsoever of distant preparation for the augmentation or maintenance of its naval force, such as the Navigation Act, bounties on the Greenland trade, and other trades regarded as nurseries for seamen.

VI., VII., VIII., IX., and X. That all these several propositions are also true of France.

As far as Great Britain is concerned, I rest the proof of these several propositions principally upon two very simple principles :—

1. That the increase of growing wealth in every nation in

a given period is necessarily limited by the quantity of capital it possesses at that period.

2. That Great Britain, with or without Ireland, and without any other dependency, can have no reasonable ground to apprehend injury from any one nation upon earth.

Turning to France, I substitute to the last of the two just-mentioned propositions the following:—

3. That France, standing singly, has at present nothing to fear from any other nation than Great Britain; nor, if standing clear of her foreign dependencies, would she have anything to fear from Great Britain.

XI. That, supposing Great Britain and France thoroughly agreed, the principal difficulties would be removed to the establishment of a plan of general and permanent pacification for all Europe.

XII. That for the maintenance of such a pacification general and perpetual treaties might be formed, limiting the number of troops to be maintained.

XIII. That the maintenance of such a pacification might be considerably facilitated by the establishment of a Common Court of Judicature for the decision of differences between the several nations, although such Court were not to be armed with any coercive powers.

XIV. That secrecy in the operations of the Foreign Department ought not to be endured in England, being altogether useless and equally repugnant to the interests of liberty and to those of peace.

PROPOSITION I.—That it is not the interest of Great Britain to have any foreign dependencies whatsoever.

The truth of this proposition will appear if we consider, first, that distant dependencies increase the chances of war:—

1. By increasing the number of possible subjects of dispute.

2. By the natural obscurity of title in case of new settlements or discoveries.

3. By the particular obscurity of the evidence resulting from the distance.

4. By men's caring less about wars when the scene is remote than when it is nearer home.

G.S.—6.   2

Secondly, that colonies are seldom, if ever, sources of profit to the mother country.

Profitable industry has five branches:—(1) Production of new materials, including agriculture, mining, and fisheries; (2) manufactures; (3) home trade; (4) foreign trade; and (5) carrying trade. The quantity of profitable industry that can be carried on in a country being limited by that of the capital which the country can command, it follows that no part of that quantity can be bestowed upon any one branch; but it must be withdrawn from, or withholden from, all the others. No encouragement, therefore, can be given to anyone, but it must be a proportionable discouragement to all the others. Nothing can be done by Government to induce a man to begin or continue to employ his capital in any one of those branches, but it must induce him in the same degree to withdraw or withhold that capital from all the rest. Of these five branches, no one is to such a degree more beneficial to the public than the rest as that it should be worth its while to call forth the powers of law to give it an advantage. But if there were any, it would unquestionably be the improvement and cultivation of land, every fictitious encouragement to any one of these rival branches being a proportionable discouragement to agriculture. Every encouragement to any of those branches of manufacture which produce articles that are at present sold to the colonies is a proportionable discouragement to agriculture.

When colonies are to be made out to be beneficial to the mother country, and the quantum of the benefit is to be estimated, the mode in which the estimate is made is curious enough. An account is taken of what they export, which is almost the whole of their produce. All this, it is said, while you have the colonies, is yours; this is exactly what you lose if you lose your colonies. How much of all this is really yours? Not one single halfpenny. When they let you take it from them, do they give it to you for nothing? Not they, indeed; they make you pay for it just as anybody else would do. How much? Just so much as you would pay them if they belonged to themselves or to anybody else.

For maintaining colonies there are several avowed reasons, besides others which are not avowed: of the avowed reasons,

oy far the principal one is the benefit of trade. If your colonies were not subject to you, they would not trade with you; they would not buy any of your goods, or let you buy any of theirs; at least, you could not be sure of their doing so: if they were subject to anybody else they would not do so, for the colonies of other nations are, you see, not suffered to trade with you. Give up your colonies and you give up so much of your trade as is carried on with your colonies. No, we do not give up any such 'thing—we do not give up anything whatsoever. Trade with colonies cannot, any more than with anywhere else, be carried on without capital: just so much of our capital as is employed in our trade with the colonies—just so much of it is not employed elsewhere—just so much is either kept or taken from other trades.

Suppose, then, any branch of trade or manufacture to decline —even suppose it lost altogether—is this any permanent loss to the nation? Not the smallest. We know the worst that can happen from any such loss; the capital that would otherwise have been employed in the lost branch will be employed in agriculture. The loss of the colonies, if the loss of the colony trade were the consequence of the loss of the colonies, would at the worst be so much gain to agriculture.

Other reasons against distant dominion may be found in a consideration of the good of the Government. Distant mischiefs make little impression on those on whom the remedying of them depends. A single murder committed in London makes more impression than if thousands of murders and other cruelties were committed in the East Indies. The situation of Hastings, only because he was present, excited compassion in those who heard the detail of the cruelties committed by him with indifference.

The communication of grievances cannot be too quick from those who feel them to those who have the power to relieve them. The reason which in the old writs the King is made to assign for his interfering to afford relief is the real cause which originally gave birth to that interference—it is one of those few truths which have contrived to make their way through the thick cloud of lies and nonsense they contain. " See what it is that these people want," says the Sovereign to the ministers of justice, " that I may not any more be troubled with their noise."

The motive assigned to the unjust Judge in the Gospel is the motive which the Sovereign, who is styled the fountain of justice, is thus made to avow.

The following, then, are the final measures which ought to be pursued :—

1. Give up all the colonies.

2. Found no new colonies.

The following is a summary of the reasons for giving up all the colonies :—

I. Interest of the mother country.

1. Saving the expense of the establishments, civil and military.

2. Saving the danger of war (a) For enforcing their obedience; (b) on account of the jealousy produced by the apparent power they confer.

3. Saving the expense of defending them in case of war on other grounds.

4. Getting rid of the means of corruption afforded by the patronage (a) of their civil establishments; (b) of the military force employed in their defence.

5. Simplifying the whole frame of government, and thereby rendering a competent skill in the business of government more attainable (a) to the members of administration; (b) to the people (b).

(b) Reasons for giving up Gibraltar :—

1. The expense of the military establishment, viz., fortifications, garrisons, ordnance, recruiting service, and victualling.

2. The means of corruption resulting from the patronage.

3. The saving of the danger of war with Spain, to which the possession of the place is a perpetual provocation.

4. The price that might be obtained from Spain for the purchase of it.

5. Saving the occasional expense of defending it and victualling it in war.

6. The possession of it is useless. It is said to be useful only on account of the Levant trade. But (1) we could carry on that trade equally well without Gibraltar. (2) If we could not, we should suffer no loss; the capital employed in that trade would be equally productive if employed in any other. (3) Supposing this the most productive of all trades, yet what we lost by losing Gibraltar would only be equal to the difference between the percentage gained in that trade and the percentage gained in the next most productive trade. For (4) we could still do as the Swedes, Danes, Dutch, &c., and as we did before we had possession of Gibraltar.

Reasons for giving up the East Indies :—

1. Saving the danger of war.

2. Getting rid of the means of corruption resulting from the patronage, civil and military.

3. Simplifying the government.

The stock of national intelligence is deteriorated by the false notions which must be kept up, in order to prevent the nation from opening its eyes and insisting upon the enfranchisement of the colonies.

At the same time bad government results to the mother country from the complication of interests, the indistinct views, and the consumption of time occasioned by the load of distant dependencies.

II. Interest of the colonies.

Diminishing the chance of bad government resulting from (1) opposite interest; (2) ignorance.

The real interests of the colony must be sacrificed to the imaginary interests of the mother country. It is for the purpose of governing it badly, and for no other, that you can wish to get or to keep a colony. Govern it well, it is of no use to you. Govern it as well as the inhabitants would govern it themselves —you must choose those to govern it whom they themselves would choose. You must sacrifice none of its interests to your own—you must bestow as much time and attention to their interests as they would themselves; in a word, you must take those very measures, and none others, which they themselves would take. But would this be governing? And what would it be worth to you if it were?

After all, it would be impossible for you to govern them so well as they would govern themselves on account of the distance (c).

The following are approximating measures:—

1. Maintain no military force in any of the colonies.

2. Issue no moneys for the maintenance of any civil establishment in any of the colonies.

3. Nominate to the offices in the colonies as long as they permit you; yield as soon as they contest such nomination.

---

4. Getting rid of prosecutions that consume the time of Parliament and beget suspicion of injustice.

5. Preventing the corruption of the morals of the natives by the example of successful rapacity.

(c) It is in proportion as we see things—as they are brought within the reach of our attention and observation—that we care for them. A Minister who would not kill one man with his own hands does not mind causing the death of myriads by the hands of others at a distance.

4. Give general instructions to governors to consent to all acts presented to them.

5. Issue no moneys for fortifications.

PROPOSITION II.—That it is not the interest of Great Britain to have any treaty of alliance, offensive or defensive, with any other Power whatsoever.

Reason: saving the danger of war arising out of them.

And more especially ought not Great Britain to guarantee foreign Constitutions.

Reason: saving the danger of war resulting from the odium of so tyrannical a measure.

PROPOSITION III.—That it is not the interest of Great Britain to have any treaty with any Power whatsoever for the purpose of possessing any advantages whatsoever, in point of trade, to the exclusion of any other nation whatsoever.

That the trade of every nation is limited by the quantity of capital is so plainly and obviously true as to challenge a place among self-evident propositions. But self-evident propositions must not expect to be easily admitted, if admitted at all, if the consequences of them clash with prevalent passions and confirmed prejudices.

Nations are composed of individuals. The trade of a nation must be limited by the same causes that limit the trade of the individual. Each individual merchant, when he has as much trade as his whole capital, and all the credit he can get by means of his capital can suffice for carrying on, can have no more. This being true of each merchant, is not less true of the whole number of merchants put together.

Many books directly recognise the proposition, that the quantity of trade a nation can carry on is limited—limited by the quantity of its capital. None dispute the proposition; but almost all, somewhere or other, proceed upon the opposite supposition; they suppose the quantity of trade to have no limitation whatsoever.

It is a folly to buy manufactured goods, wise to buy raw materials. Why? Because you sell them to yourselves, or, what is still better, to foreigners, manufactured; and the manufacturer's profit is all clear gain to you. What is here forgotten is,

that the manufacturer, to carry on his business, must have a capital; and that just so much capital as is employed in that way is prevented from being employed in any other.

Hence the perfect inutility and mischievousness of all laws and public measures of government whatsoever, for the pretended encouragement of trade—all bounties in every shape whatsoever —all non-importation agreements and engagements to consume home manufactures in preference to foreign—in any other view than to afford temporary relief to temporary distress.

But of the two—prohibitions and bounties, penal encouragements and remuneratory—the latter are beyond comparison the most mischievous. Prohibitions, except while they are fresh and drive men at a great expense out of the employments they are embarked in, are only nugatory. Bounties are wasteful and oppressive: they force money from one man in order to pay another man for carrying on a trade, which, if it were not a losing one, there would be no need of paying him for.

What, then, are all modes of productive industry alike? May not one be more profitable than another? Certainly. But the favourite one—is it, in fact, more profitable than any other? That is the question and the only question that ought to be put; and that is the very question which nobody ever thinks of putting.

Were it ever put and answered, and answered ever so clearly, it never could be of any use as a ground for any permanent plan of policy. Why? Because almost as soon as one branch is known to be more profitable than the rest, so soon it ceases so to be. Men flock to it from all other branches, and the old equilibrium is presently restored. Your merchants have a monopoly as against foreigners? True, but they have no monopoly as against one another. Men cannot, in every instance, quit the less productive branch their capitals are already employed in, to throw them into this more productive one? True—but there are young beginners as well as old stagers; and the first concern of a young beginner, who has a capital to employ in a branch of industry, is to look out for the most profitable.

Objection:—Oh! but it is manufacture that creates the demand for the productions of agriculture. You cannot, therefore, increase the productions of agriculture but by increasing manufactures. No such thing. I admit the antecedent—I deny the

consequence. Increase of manufactures certainly does create an increase in the demand for the productions of agriculture. Equally certain is it that the increase of manufactures is not necessary to produce an increase in that demand. Farmers can subsist without ribbons, gauzes, or fine cambrics. Weavers of ribbons, gauzes, or fine cambrics cannot subsist without the production of agriculture; necessary subsistence never can lose its value. Those who produce it are themselves a market for their produce. Is it possible that provisions should be too cheap? Is there any present danger of it? Suppose (in spite of the extreme absurdity of the supposition) that provisions were growing gradually too cheap, from the increase of the quantity produced, and the want of manufacturers to consume them, what would be the consequence? The increasing cheapness would increase the facility and disposition to marry: it would thence increase the population of the country; and the children thus produced, eating as they grew up, would keep down this terrible evil of a superabundance of provisions.

Provisions, the produce of agriculture, constantly and necessarily produce a market for themselves. The more provisions a man raises, over and above what is necessary for his own consumption, the more he has to give to others, to induce them to provide him with whatever, besides provisions, he chooses to have. In a word, the more he has to spare, the more he has to give to manufacturers; who, by taking it from him, and paying him with the produce of their labours, afford the encouragement requisite for the productions of the fruits of agriculture.

It is impossible, therefore, that you can ever have too much agriculture. It is impossible that while there is ground untilled, or ground that might be better tilled than it is, that any detriment should ensue to the community from the withholding or withdrawing capital from any other branch of industry, and employing it in agriculture. It is impossible, therefore, that the loss of any branch of trade can be productive of any detriment to the community, excepting always the temporary distress experienced by the individuals concerned in it for the time being, when the decline is a sudden one.

The following are the measures the propriety of which results from the above principles :—

1. That no treaties granting commercial preferences should be made.

2. That no wars should be entered into for compelling such treaties.

3. That no alliances should be contracted for the sake of purchasing them.

4. That no encouragement should be given to particular branches of trade, by—

(a) Prohibition of rival manufactures.

(b) Taxation of rival manufactures.

(c) Bounties on the trade meant to be favoured (d).

5. That no treaties should be entered into insuring commercial preferences.

They are useless as they add nothing to the mass of wealth; they only influence the direction of it.

PROPOSITION IV.—That it is not the interest of Great Britain to keep up any naval force beyond what may be sufficient to defend its commerce against pirates.

It is unnecessary, except for the defence of the colonies, or for the purposes of war, undertaken either for the compelling of trade or the formation of commercial treaties.

PROPOSITION V.—That it is not the interest of Great Britain to keep on foot any regulations whatsoever of distant preparation for the augmentation or maintenance of its naval force, such as the Navigation Act, bounties on the Greenland trade, and other trades regarded as nurseries for seamen.

This proposition is a necessary consequence of the foregoing one.

PROPOSITIONS VI., VII., VIII., IX. and X.

Propositions similar to the foregoing are equally true applied to France.

PROPOSITION XI.—That supposing Great Britain and France thoroughly agreed, the principal difficulties would be removed to the establishment of a plan of general and permanent pacification for all Europe.

(d) All bounties on particular branches of trade do rather harm than good

PROPOSITION XII.—That for the maintenance of such a pacification, general and perpetual treaties might be formed, limiting the number of troops to be maintained (e).

If the simple relation of a single nation with a single other nation be considered, perhaps the matter would not be very difficult. The misfortune is, that almost everywhere compound relations are found. On the subject of troops, France says to England: Yes, I would voluntarily make with you a treaty of disarming, if there were only you; but it is necessary for me to have troops to defend me from the Austrians. Austria might say the same to France; but it is necessary to guard against Prussia, Russia, and the Porte. And the like allegation might be made by Prussia with regard to Russia.

Whilst as to naval forces, if it concerned Europe only, the difficulty might perhaps not be very considerable. To consider France, Spain and Holland as making together a counterpoise to the power of Britain—perhaps on account of the disadvantages which accompany the concert between three separate nations, to say nothing of the tardiness and publicity of procedures under the Dutch Constitution—perhaps England might allow to all together a united force equal to half or more than its own.

An agreement of this kind would not be dishonourable. If the covenant were on one side only, it might be so. If it regard both parties together, the reciprocity takes away the acerbity. By the treaty which put an end to the first Punic war, the number of vessels that the Carthaginians might maintain was limited. This condition, was it not humiliating? It might be: but if it were, it must have been because there was nothing correspondent to it on the side of the Romans. A treaty which placed all the security on one side—what cause could it have had for its source? It could only have had one, that is, the avowed superiority of the party thus incontestably secured; such a condition could only have been a law dictated by the conqueror to the party conquered—the law of the strongest. None but a conqueror could have dictated it; none but the conquered would have accepted it.

(e) Precedents :   (1) Convention of disarmament between France and Britain, 1787—this is a precedent of the measure or stipulation itself. (2) Armed neutrality code—this is a precedent of the mode of bringing about the measure, and may serve to disprove the impossibility of a general Convention among nations. (3) Treaty forbidding the fortifying of Dunkirk.

On the contrary, whatsoever nation should get the start of the other in making the proposal to reduce and fix the amount of its armed force would crown itself with everlasting honour. The risk would be nothing—the gain certain. This gain would be the giving an incontrovertible demonstration of its own disposition to peace, and of the opposite disposition in the other nation in case of its rejecting the proposal.

The utmost fairness should be employed. The nation addressed should be invited to consider and point out whatever further securities it deemed necessary, and whatever further concessions it deemed just.

The proposal should be made in the most public manner: it should be an address from nation to nation. This, at the same time that it conciliated the confidence of the nation addressed, would make it impracticable for the Government of that nation to neglect it, or stave it off by shifts and evasions. It would sound the heart of the nation addressed. It would discover its intentions and proclaim them to the world.

The cause of humanity has still another resource. Should Britain prove deaf and impracticable, let France, without conditions, emancipate her colonies, and break up her marine. The advantage even upon this plan would be immense, the danger none. The colonies I have already shown are a source of expense, not of revenue: of burthen to the people, not of relief. This appears to be the case, even upon the footing of those expenses which appear upon the face of them to belong to the colonies, and are the only ones that have hitherto been set down to their account. But in fact the whole expense of the marine belongs also to that account, and no other. What other destination has it? What other can it have? None. Take away the colonies, what use would there be for a single vessel, more than the few necessary in the Mediterranean to curb the pirates.

In case of a war, where at present (1789) would England make its first and only attack upon France? In the colonies. What would she propose to herself from success in such an attack? What but the depriving France of her colonies. Were these colonies—these bones of contention—no longer hers, what then could England do? What could she wish to do?

There would remain the territory of France; with what view

could Britain make any attack upon it in any way? Not with views of permanent conquest—such madness does not belong to our age. Parliament itself, one may venture to affirm, without paying it any very extraordinary compliment, would not wish it. It would not wish it, even could it be accomplished without effort on our part, without resistance on the other. It would not, even though France herself were to solicit it. No Parliament would grant a penny for such a purpose. If it did, it would not be a Parliament a month. No King would lend his name to such a project. He would be dethroned as surely and as deservedly as James the Second. To say, I will be King of France, would be to say, in other words, I will be absolute in England.

Well, then, no one would dream of conquest. What other purpose could an invasion have? The plunder and destruction of the country. Such baseness is totally repugnant, not only to the spirit of the nation, but to the spirit of the times. Malevolence could be the only motive—rapacity could never counsel it; long before an army could arrive anywhere everything capable of being plundered would be carried off. Whatever is portable could be much sooner carried off by the owners than by any plundering army. No expedition of plunder could ever pay itself (f).

Such is the extreme folly, the madness of war: on no supposition can it be otherwise than mischievous, especially between nations circumstanced as France and England. Though the choice of the events were absolutely at your command, you could not make it of use to you. If unsuccessful, you may be disgraced and ruined: if successful, even to the height of your wishes, you are still but so much the worse. You would still be so much the worse, though it were to cost you nothing. For not even any

---

(f) This brings to recollection the achievements of the war from 1755 to 1763. The struggle betwixt prejudice and humanity produced in conduct a result truly ridiculous. Prejudice prescribed an attack upon the enemy in his own territory; humanity forbade the doing him any harm. Not only nothing was gained by these expeditions, but the mischief done to the country invaded was not nearly equal to the expense of the invasion. When a Japanese rips open his own belly, it is in the assurance that his enemy will follow his example. But in this instance the Englishman ripped open his own belly that the Frenchman might get a scratch. Why was this absurdity acted? Because we were at war; and when nations are at war something must be done, or at least appear to be done, and there was nothing else to be done. France was already stripped of all its distant dependencies.

colony of your own planting, still less a conquest of your own making, will so much as pay its own expenses.

The greatest acquisitions that could be conceived would not be to be wished for—could they even be attained with the greatest certainty and without the least expense. In war, we are as likely not to gain as to gain—as likely to lose as to do either: we can neither attempt the one, nor defend ourselves against the other, without a certain and most enormous expense.

Mark well the contrast. All trade is in its essence advantageous—even to that party to whom it is least so. All war is in its essence ruinous; and yet the great employments of government are to treasure up occasions of war, and to put fetters upon trade.

Ask an Englishman what is the great obstacle to a secure and solid peace, he has his answer ready: It is the ambition, perhaps he will add the treachery, of France. I wish the chief obstacle to a plan for this purpose were the dispositions and sentiments of France. Were that all, the plan need not long wait for adoption!

Of this visionary project, the most visionary part is without question that for the emancipation of distant dependencies. What will an Englishman say, when he sees two French Ministers (g) of the highest reputation, both at the head of their respective departments, both joining in the opinion that the accomplishment of this event, nay, the speedy accomplishment of it, is inevitable, and one of them scrupling not to pronounce it as eminently desirable.

It would only be bringing things back on these points to the footing they were on before the discovery of America. Europe had then no colonies, no distant garrisons, no standing armies. It would have had no wars but for the feudal system, religious antipathy, the rage of conquest, and the uncertainties of succession. Of these four causes, the first is happily extinct everywhere, the second and third almost everywhere—and at any rate in France and England—the last might, if not already extinguished, be so with great ease.

(g) Turgot and Vergennes.

The moral feelings of men in matters of national morality are still so far short of perfection that, in the scale of estimation, justice has not yet gained the ascendency over force. Yet this prejudice may, in a certain point of view, by accident, be rather favourable to this proposal rather than otherwise. Truth, and the object of this essay, bid me to say to my countrymen, it is for you to begin the reformation—it is you that have been the greatest sinners. But the same considerations also lead me to say to them, you are the strongest among nations : though justice be not on your side, force is; and it is your force that has been the main cause of your injustice. If the measure of moral approbation had been brought to perfection, such positions would have been far from popular, prudence would have dictated the keeping them out of sight, and the softening them down as much as possible.

Humiliation would have been the effect produced by them on those to whom they appeared true—indignation on those to whom they appeared false. But, as I have observed, men have not yet learned to tune their feelings in unison with the voice of morality in these points. They feel more pride in being accounted strong than resentment at being called unjust: or, rather, the imputation of injustice appears flattering rather than otherwise when coupled with the consideration of its cause. I feel it in my own experience; but if I, listed as I am as the professed and hitherto the only advocate in my own country in the cause of justice, set a less value on justice than is its due, what can I expect from the general run of men?

Proposition XIII.—That the maintenance of such a pacification might be considerably facilitated by the establishment of a Common Court of Judicature for the decision of differences between the several nations, although such Court were not to be armed with any coercive powers.

It is an observation of somebody's, that no nation ought to yield any evident point of justice to another. This must mean evident in the eyes of the nation that is to judge—evident in the eyes of the nation called upon to yield. What does this amount to? That no nation is to give up anything of what it looks upon as its rights—no nation is to make any concessions. Wherever

there is any difference of opinion between the negotiators of two nations, war is to be the consequence.

While there is no common tribunal, something might be said for this. Concession to notorious injustice invites fresh injustice.

Establish a common tribunal, the necessity for war no longer follows from difference of opinion. Just or unjust, the decision of the arbiters will save the credit, the honour of the contending party.

Can the arrangement proposed be justly styled visionary, when it has been proved of it that—

1. It is in the interest of the parties concerned.

2. They are already sensible of that interest.

3. The situation it would place them in is no new one, nor any other than the original situation they set out from.

Difficult and complicated conventions have been effectuated: for examples, we may mention—

1. The Armed Neutrality.

2. The American Confederation.

3. The German Diet.

4. The Swiss League.

Why should not the European fraternity subsist, as well as the German Diet or the Swiss League? These latter have no ambitious views. Be it so; but is not this already become the case with the former?

How then shall we concentrate the approbation of the people, and obviate their prejudices?

One main object of the plan is to effectuate a reduction, and that a mighty one, in the contributions of the people. The amount of the reduction for each nation should be stipulated in the treaty; and even previous to the signature of it, laws for the purpose might be prepared in each nation, and presented to every other, ready to be enacted as soon as the treaty should be ratified in each State.

By these means the mass of the people—the part most exposed to be led away by prejudices—would not be sooner apprised of the measure than they would feel the relief it brought them. They would see it was for their advantage it was calculated, and that it could not be calculated for any other purpose.

The concurrence of all the Maritime Powers, except England,

upon a former occasion, proved two points—the reasonableness of that measure itself, and the weakness of France in comparison with England. It was a measure, not of ambition, but of justice—a law made in favour of equality, a law made for the benefit of the weak. No sinister point was gained, or attempted to be gained, by it. France was satisfied with it. Why? Because she was weaker than Britain. She could have no other motive; on no other supposition could it have been of any advantage to her. Britain was vexed at it. Why? For the opposite reason—she could have no other.

Oh, my countrymen, purge your eyes from the film of prejudice; extirpate from your hearts the *black specks* of excessive jealousy, false ambition, selfishness, and insolence! The operations may be painful, but the rewards are glorious indeed. As the main difficulty, so will the main honour be with you.

What though wars should hereafter arise? The intermediate savings will not the less be so much clear gain.

Though in the generating of the disposition of war, unjust ambition has doubtless had by far too great a share, yet jealousy, sincere and honest jealousy, must be acknowledged to have had a not inconsiderable one. Vulgar prejudice, fostered by passion, assigns the heart as the seat of all the moral diseases it complains of. But the principal and more frequent seat is really the head; it is from ignorance and weakness that men deviate from the path of rectitude more frequently than from selfishness and malevolence. This is fortunate; for the power of information and reason over error and ignorance is much greater and much surer than that of exhortation and all the modes of rhetoric over selfishness and malevolence.

It is because we do not know what strong motives other nations have to be just, what strong indications they have given of the disposition to be so—how often we ourselves have deviated from the rules of justice—that we take for granted, as an indisputable truth, that the principles of injustice are in a manner interwoven into the very essence of the hearts of other men.

The diffidence which forms part of the character of the English nation may have been one cause of this jealousy. The dread of being duped by other nations—the notion that foreign heads are more able, though at the same time foreign hearts

are less honest, than our own—has always been one of our prevailing weaknesses. This diffidence has, perhaps, some connection with the *mauvaise honte* which has been remarked as commonly showing itself in our behaviour, and which makes public speaking and public exhibition in every line a task so much more formidable to us than to other people.

This diffidence may, perhaps, in part be accounted for from our living less in society and accustoming ourselves less to mixed companies than the people of other nations.

But the particular cast of diffidence in question—the apprehension of being duped by foreign Powers—is to be referred in part, and perhaps principally, to another cause—the jealousy and slight opinion we entertain of our Ministers and public men. We are jealous of them as our superiors, contending against us in the perpetual struggle for power; we are diffident of them as being our fellow-countrymen, and of the same mould as ourselves.

Jealousy is the vice of narrow minds; confidence the virtue of enlarged ones. To be satisfied that confidence between nations is not out of nature where they have worthy Ministers, one need but read the account of the negotiation between De Wit and Temple as given by Hume. I say by Hume—for as it required negotiators like De Wit and Temple to carry on such a negotiation in such a manner, so it required a historian like Hume to do it justice. For the vulgar among historians know no other receipt for writing that part of history than the finding out whatever are the vilest and basest motives capable of accounting for men's conduct in the situation in question, and then ascribing it to those motives without ceremony and without proof.

Temple and De Wit, whose confidence in each other was so exemplary and so just; Temple and De Wit were two of the wisest, as well as most honourable, men in Europe. The age which produced such virtue was, however, the age of the pretended Popish plot, and of a thousand other enormities which cannot now be thought of without horror. Since then the world has had upwards of a century to improve itself in experience, in reflection, in virtue. In every other line its improvements have been immense and unquestioned. Is it too much to hope that France and England might produce, not a Temple and a

De Wit—virtue so transcendent as theirs would not be necessary —but men who, in happier times, might achieve a work like theirs with less extent of virtue?

Such a Congress or Diet might be constituted by each Power sending two deputies to the place of meeting, one of these to be the principal, the other to act as an occasional substitute.

The proceedings of such Congress or Diet should be all public.

Its power would consist (1) in reporting its opinion;

(2) in causing that opinion to be circulated in the dominions of each State.

Manifestos are in common usage. A manifesto is designed to be read either by the subjects of the State complained of, or by other States, or by both. It is an appeal to them. It calls for their opinion. The difference is that in that case nothing of proof is given; no opinion regularly made known.

The example of Sweden is alone sufficient to show the influence which treaties, the acts of nations, may be expected to have over the subjects of the several nations, and how far the expedient in question deserves the character of a weak one, or the proposal for employing and trusting to it that of a visionary proposal.

The war commenced by the King of Sweden against Russia was deemed by his subjects, or at least a considerable part of them, offensive, and, as such, contrary to the Constitution established by him with the concurrence of the States. Hence a considerable part of the army either threw up their commissions or refused to act, and the consequence was the King was obliged to retreat from the Russian frontier and call a Diet.

This was under a Government commonly, though not truly, supposed to be changed from a limited monarchy, or rather aristocracy, to a despotic monarchy. There was no act of any recognised and respected tribunal to guide and fix the opinion of the people. The only document they had to judge from was a manifesto of the enemy couched in terms such as resentment would naturally dictate, and therefore none of the most conciliating—a document which had no claim to be circulated, and of which the circulation, we may be pretty well assured, was

prevented as much as it was in the power of the utmost vigilance of the Government to prevent it.

(3) After a certain time, in putting the refractory State under the ban of Europe.

There might, perhaps, be no harm in regulating, as a last resource, the contingent to be furnished by the several States for enforcing the decrees of the Court. But the necessity for the employment of this resource would, in all human probability, be superseded for ever by having recourse to the much more simple and less burthensome expedient of introducing into the instrument by which such Court was instituted a clause guaranteeing the liberty of the Press in each State, in such sort that the Diet might find no obstacle to its giving, in every State, to its decrees and to every paper whatever, which it might think proper to sanction with its signature, the most extensive and unlimited circulation.

PROPOSITION XIV.—That secrecy in the operations of the Foreign Department in England ought not to be endured, being altogether useless and equally repugnant to the interests of liberty and peace.

The existence of the rule which throws a veil of secrecy over the transactions of the Cabinet with foreign Powers I shall not take upon me to dispute. My objection is to the propriety of it.

Being asked in the House of Lords by Lord Stormont (h) about secret Articles, the Minister for Foreign Affairs refuses to answer. I blame him not. Subsisting rules, it seems to be agreed, forbid reply. They throw a general veil of secrecy over the transactions of the Cabinet with foreign Powers. I blame no man for the fault of the laws. It is these laws that I blame as repugnant to the spirit of the Constitution and incompatable with good government.

I take at once the boldest and the broadest ground. I lay down two propositions : —

1. That in no negotiation, and at no period of any negotiation, ought the negotiations of the Cabinet in this country to be kept

---

(h) May 22, 1789.

secret from the public at large, much less from Parliament and after inquiry made in Parliament (i).

2. That whatever may be the case with preliminary negotiations, such secrecy ought never to be maintained with regard to treaties actually concluded.

In both cases, to a country like this, such secrecy is equally mischievous and unnecessary.

It is mischievous. Over measures of which you have no knowledge you can apply no control. Measures carried on without your knowledge you cannot stop, how ruinous soever to you, and how strongly soever you would disapprove of them if you knew them. Of negotiations with foreign Powers carried on in time of peace, the principal terminations are treaties of alliance, offensive or defensive, or treaties of commerce. But by one accident or other everything may lead to war.

That in new treaties of commerce, as such, there can be no cause for secrecy is a proposition that will hardly be disputed. Only such negotiations, like all others, may eventually lead to war; and everything connected with war, it will be said, may come to require secrecy.

But rules which admit of a Minister's plunging the nation into a war against its will are essentially mischievous and unconstitutional.

It is admitted that Ministers ought not to have it in their power to impose taxes on the nation against its will. It is admitted that they ought not to have it in their power to maintain troops against its will. But by plunging it into war without its knowledge they do both.

Parliament may refuse to carry on a war after it is begun. Parliament may remove and punish the Minister who has brought the nation into a war.

Sorry remedies these. Add them both together, their efficacy is not worth a straw. Arrestment of the evil and punishment of the authors are sad consolations for the mischief of the war, and of no value as remedies in comparison with prevention. Aggressive war is a matter of choice: defensive, of necessity. Refusal of the means of continuing a war is a most precarious

---

(i) It lies upon the other side, at least, to put a case in which want of secrecy may produce a specific mischief.

remedy—a remedy only in name. What, when the enemy is at your doors, refuse the materials for barricading them?

Before aggression, war or no war depends upon the aggressor. Once begun, the party aggrieved acquires a vote. He has his negative upon every plan for terminating the war. What is to be done? Give yourself up without resistance to the mercy of a justly exasperated enemy? But this or the continuance of the war is all the choice that is now left. In what state of things can this remedy be made to serve? Are you unsuccessful? The remedy is inapplicable. Are you successful? Nobody will call for it.

Punishment of the authors of the war—punishment, whatever it may be, to the personal adversaries of the Ministers—is no satisfaction to the nation. This is self-evident. But what is closer to the purpose and not less true is that, in a case like this,· the fear of punishment on such an account is no check to them; of a majority in Parliament they are in possession, or they would not be Ministers. That they should be abandoned by this majority is not in the catalogue of events that ought to be looked upon as possible, but between abandoning them and punishing them there is a wide difference. Lord North was abandoned in the American War; he was not punished for it. His was an honest error in judgment, unstained by any *mala fide* practice and countenanced by a fair majority in Parliament. And so may any other impolitic and unjust war be. This is not a punishing age. If bribe-taking, oppression, peculation, duplicity, treachery, every crime that can be committed by statesmen sinning against conscience, produce no desire to punish, what dependence can be placed on punishment in a case where the mischief may so easily happen without any ground for punishment? Mankind are not yet arrived at that stage in the track of civilisation. Foreign nations are not yet considered as objects susceptible of an injury. For the citizens of other civilised nations we have not so much feeling as for our negroes. There are instances in which Ministers have been punished for making peace (*k*): there are none where they

(*k*) The fate of Queen Anne's last Ministry may be referred in some degree to this cause, and owing to the particular circumstances of their conduct they perhaps deserved it : see the Report of the Secret Committee of the

have been so much as questioned for bringing the nation into war; and if punishment had been ever applied on such an occasion it would be not for the mischief done to the foreign nation, but purely for the mischief brought upon their own— not for the injustice, but purely for the imprudence.

It has never been laid down as a rule that you should pay any regard to foreign nations; it has never been laid down that you should stick at anything which would give you an advantage in your dealings with foreign nations. On what ground could a Minister be punished for a war, even the most unsuccessful, brought on by any such means? " I did my best to serve you," he would say. " The worse the measure was for the foreign nation, the more I took upon me; the greater, therefore, the zeal I showed for your cause; the event has proved unfavourable. Are zeal and misfortune to be represented as crimes?"

A war unjust on the part of our own nation, by whose Ministers it is brought on, can never be brought on but in pursuit of some advantage which, were it not for the injustice towards the foreign nation, it would be for our interests to pursue. The injustice and the danger of retaliation being on all hands looked upon as nothing, the plea of the Minister would always be: " It was *your* interest I was pursuing." And the uninformed and unreflecting part of the nation, that is, the great body of the nation, would echo to him: " Yes, it was our interest you were preserving." The voice of the nation on these subjects can only be looked for in newspapers. But on these subjects the language of all newspapers is uniform: " It is we that are always in the right, without a possibility of being otherwise. Against us other nations have no rights. If, according to the rules of judging between individual and individual, we are right, we are right by the rules of justice : if not, we are right by the laws of patriotism, which is a virtue

---

House of Commons in the year 1715. The great crime of the Earl of Buté was making peace. The Earl of Shelburne was obliged to resign for having made peace. The great crime of Sir R. Walpole was keeping the peace. The nation was become tired of peace. Walpole was reproached with proposing half-a-million in the year for secret service money. His errors were rectified, war was made, and in one year there was laid out in war four times what he had spent in the ten years before.

more respectable than justice." Injustice, oppression, fraud, lying, whatever acts would be crimes, whatever habits would be vices, if manifested in the pursuit of individual interests when manifested in pursuit of national interests become sublimated into virtues. Let any man declare, who has ever read or heard an English newspaper, whether this be not the constant tenor of the notions they convey. Party on this one point makes no difference. However hostile to one another on all other points, on this they have never but one voice—they write with the utmost harmony. Such are the opinions, and to these opinions the facts are accommodated as of course. Who would blush to misrepresent when misrepresentation is a virtue?

But newspapers, if their voice make but a small part of the voice of the people, the instruction they give makes on these subjects the whole of the instruction which the people receive.

Such being the national propensity to error on these points, and to error on the worst side, the danger of parliamentary punishment for misconduct of this kind must appear equivalent to next to nothing, even in the eyes of an unconcerned and cool spectator. What must it appear, then, in the eyes of Ministers themselves, acting under the seduction of self-partiality, and hurried on by the tide of business? No, the language which a Minister on such occasions will hold to himself will be uniformly this: " In the first place, what I do is not wrong; in the next place, if it were, nothing should I have to fear from it."

Under the present system of secrecy Ministers have, therefore, every seduction to lead them into misconduct, while they have no check to keep them out of it. And what species of misconduct? That in comparison of which all others are but peccadillos. Let a Minister throw away £30,000 or £40,000 in pensions to his creatures. Let him embezzle a few hundred thousand for himself. What is that to fifty or a hundred millions, the ordinary burthen of a war? Observe the consequence. This is the Department of all others in which the strongest checks are needful. At the same time, thanks to the rules of secrecy of all the Departments, this is the only one in which there are no checks at all. I say, then, the conclusion is demonstrated. The principle which throws a veil of secrecy over the proceedings of the Foreign Department of the Cabinet is pernicious in the

highest degree, pregnant with mischiefs superior to everything
to which the most perfect absence of all concealment could
possibly give rise.

There still remains a sort of inexplicit notion which may
present itself as secretly furnishing an argument on the other
side. Such is the condition of the British nation. Peace and
war may be always looked upon as being to all human probability
in good measure in her power. When the worst comes to the
worst, peace may always be had by some unessential sacrifice.
I admit the force of the argument; what I maintain is that it
operates in my favour. Why? It depends upon two propositions—the matchless strength of this country, and the uselessness
of her foreign dependencies. I admit both. But both operate
as arguments in my favour. Her strength places her above
the danger of surprise, and above the necessity of having
recourse to it to defend herself. The uselessness of her foreign
dependencies proves *a fortiori* the uselessness of engaging in wars
for their protection and defence. If they are not fit to keep
without war, much less are they worth keeping at the price of
war. The inutility of a secret Cabinet is demonstrated by this
short dilemma. For offensive measures Cabinet secrecy can
never be necessary to this nation; for defence it can never be
necessary to any.

My persuasion is that there is no State whatever in which
any inconveniences capable of arising from publicity in this
Department would not be greatly overbalanced by the advantages,
be the State ever so great or ever so small, ever so strong or
ever so weak, be its form of government pure or mixed, single
or confederated, monarchical, aristocratical, or democratical.
The observations already given seem in all these cases sufficient
to warrant the conclusion.

But in a nation like Britain the safety of publicity, the
inutility of secrecy in all such business, stands upon peculiar
grounds. Stronger than any other two nations, much stronger,
of course, than any *one*, its superiority deprives it of all pretence
of necessity of carrying points by surprise. Clandestine surprise
is the resource of knavery and fear, of unjust ambition combined
with weakness. Her matchless power exempts her from the

one; her interest, if her servants could be brought to be governed by her evident interests, would forbid the other.

Taking the interest of the first servant of the State, as distinct from, and opposite to, the nation, clandestinity may undoubtedly be, in certain cases, favourable to the projects of sceptred thieves and robbers. Without taking the precautions of a thief, the Great Frederic might probably enough not have succeeded in the enterprise of stealing Silesia from her lawful Sovereign. Without an advantage of this sort, the triple gang might, perhaps, not have found it quite so easy to secure what they stole from Poland. Whether there can or cannot exist occasions on which it might, in this point of view, be the interest of a King of Great Britain to turn highwayman is a question I shall waive; but a proposition I shall not flinch from is, that it never can be the interest of the nation to abet him in it. When those sceptred sinners sold themselves to the service of Mammon, they did not serve him for naught; the booty was all their own. Were we (I speak as one of the body of the nation) to assist our King in committing a robbery upon France, the booty would be his. He would have the naming of the new places, which is all the value that in the hands of a British robber such booty can be to anybody. The privilege of paying for the horse and pistols is all that would be ours. The booty would be employed in corrupting our confidential servants, and this is the full and exact amount of what we should get by it.

Conquests made by New Zealanders have some sense in them. While the conquered fry the conquerors fatten. Conquests made by the polished nations of antiquity—conquests made by Greeks and Romans—had some sense in them. Lands, movables, inhabitants, everything, went into the pocket. The invasions of France in the days of the Edwards and the Henrys had a rational object. Prisoners were taken, and the country was stripped to pay their ransom. The ransom of a single prisoner, a Duke of Orleans, exceeded one-third of the national revenue of England.

Conquests made by a modern despot of the Continent have still some sense in them. The new property, being contiguous, is laid on to his old property; the inhabitants, as many as he thinks fit to set his mark upon, go to increase his armies; their

substance, as much as he thinks fit to squeeze from them, goes into his purse.

Conquests made by the British nation would be violations of common sense, were there no such thing as justice. They are bungling imitations of miserable originals, bating the essential circumstances. Nothing but confirmed blindness and stupidity can prompt us to go on imitating Alexander and Cæsar, and the New Zealanders, and Catherine and Frederic, without the profit.

If it be the King alone who gets the appointment to the places, it is a part of the nation, it may be said, that gets the benefit of filling them. A precious lottery! Fifty or one hundred millions the cost of the tickets: so many years' purchase of ten or twenty thousand a year the value of the prizes. This if the scheme succeed. What if it fail?

I do not say there are no sharers in the plunder; it is impossible for the head of a gang to put the whole of it into his own pocket. All I contend for is that robbery by wholesale is not so profitable as by retail. If the whole gang together pick the pockets of strangers to a certain amount, the ringleaders pick the pockets of the rest to a much greater. Shall I, or shall I not, succeed in persuading my countrymen that it is not their interest to be thieves?

" Oh, but you mistake," cries somebody. " We do not now make war for conquests, but for trade." More foolish still. This is a still worse bargain than before. Conquer the whole world, it is impossible you should increase your trade one half-penny; it is impossible you should do otherwise than diminish it. Conquer little or much, you pay for it by taxes; but just so much as a merchant pays in taxes, just so much he is disabled from adding to the capital he employs in trade. Had you two worlds to trade with, you could only trade with them to the amount of your capital, and what credit you might meet with on the strength of it. This, being true of each trader, is so of all traders. Find a fallacy in this short argument if you can. If you obtained your new right of trading given you for nothing, you would not be a halfpenny the richer. If you paid for it by war or preparations for war, by just so much as you paid for these you would be the poorer.

The good people of England, along with the right of self-government, conquered prodigious right of trade. The revolution was to produce for them, not only the blessings of security and power, but immense and sudden wealth. Year has followed after year, and to their endless astonishment the progress to wealth has gone on no faster than before. One piece of good fortune still wanting they have never thought of—that on the day their shackles were knocked off some kind sylph should have slipped a few thousand pounds into every man's pocket. There is no law against my flying to the moon. Yet I cannot get there. Why? Because I have no wings. What wings are to flying, capital is to trade.

There are two ways of making war for trade—forcing independent nations to let you trade with them, and conquering nations, or pieces of nations, to make them trade with you. The former contrivance is to appearance the more easy, and the policy of it the more refined. The latter is more in the good old way, and the King does his own business and the nation's at the same time. He gets the naming to the places; and the nation cannot choose but join with him, being assured that it is all for the sake of getting them the trade. The places he lays hold of, good man, only out of necessity, and that they may not go a-begging; on his own account he has no more mind for them than a new-made bishop for the mitre, or a new-made speaker for the chair. To the increase of trade both these plans of war equally contribute. What you get in both cases is the pleasure of the war.

The legal right of trading to part of America was conquered by France from Britain in the last war. What have they got by it? They have got Tobago, bankruptcy, and a revolution for their fifty millions. Ministers, who to account for the bankruptcy are forced to say something about the war, call it a national one. The King has not got by it, therefore the nation has. What has it got? A fine trade, were there but capital to carry it on. With such room for trade, how comes there to be no more of it? This is what merchants and manufacturers are putting themselves to the torture to account for. The sylph so necessary elsewhere was still more necessary to France, since,

over and above her other work, there was the fifty millions spent in powder and shot to replace.

The King of France, however, by getting Tobago, probably obtained two or three thousand pounds' worth of places to give away. This is what he got, and this is all that anybody got for the nation's fifty millions. Let us go on as we have begun, strike a bold stroke, take all their vessels we can lay hold of without a declaration of war, and who knows but what we may get it back again. With the advantages we now have over them, five times the success they are so pleased with would be but a moderate expectation. For every fifty millions thus laid out our King would get in places to the amount, not of two or three thousand pounds only, but, say, of ten, fifteen, or twenty thousand pounds. All this would be prodigious glory, and fine paragraphs and speeches, thanksgiving and birthday odes might be sung and said for it; but for economy I would much rather give the King new places to the same amount at home, if at this price his Ministers would sell us peace.

The conclusion is that, as we have nothing to fear from any other nation or nations, nor want anything from other nations, we can have nothing to say to other nations, nor to hear from them, that might not be as public as any laws. What, then, is the veil of secrecy that enwraps the proceedings of the Cabinet? A mere cloak for wickedness and folly; a dispensation to Ministers to save them from the trouble of thinking; a warrant for playing all manner of mad and silly pranks, unseen and uncontrolled; a licence to play at hazard with their fellows abroad, staking our lives and fortunes upon the throw.

What, then, is the true use and effect of secrecy? That the prerogatives of place may furnish an aliment to petty vanity; that the members of *the circulation* may have, as it were, a newspaper to themselves; that under favour of the monopoly, ignorance and incapacity may put on airs of wisdom; that a man, unable to write or speak what is fit to be put into a newspaper, may toss up his head and say, " I don't read newspapers," as if a parent were to say, " I don't trouble my head about schoolmasters "; and that a Minister, secure from scrutiny in that quarter, may have the convenient opportunity, upon occasion, of filling the posts with obsequious cyphers

instead of effective men. Anything will do to make a Minister whose writing may be written for him, and whose duty in speaking consists in silence.

This much must be confessed. If secrecy, as against the nation, be useless and pernicious to the nation, it is not useless and· pernicious with regard to its servants. It forms part of the *douceurs* of office—a perquisite which will be valued in proportion to the insignificance of their characters and the narrowness of their views. It serves to pamper them up with notions of their own importance, and to teach the servants of the people to look down upon their masters.

Oh! But if everything that were written were liable to be made public—were published—who would treat with you abroad? Just the same persons as treat with you at present. Negotiations, for fear of misrepresentation, would perhaps be committed somewhat more to writing than at present. And where would be the harm? The King and his Ministers might not have quite such copious accounts, true or false, of the tittle-tattle of each Court, or they must put into different hands the tittle-tattle and the real business. And suppose your head servants were not so minutely acquainted with the mistresses and buffoons of Kings and their Ministers, what matters it to you as a nation, who have no intrigues to carry on, no petty points to compass?

It were an endless task to fill more pages with the shadows that might be conjured up in order to be knocked down. I leave that task to any that will undertake it. I challenge party men, I invite the impartial lovers of their country and mankind, to discuss the question, to ransack the stores of history and imagination as well as history, for cases, actual or possible, in which the want of secrecy in this line of business can be shown to be attended with any substantial prejudice.

As to the Constitution, the question of Cabinet secrecy has never been tried by the principles of the Constitution—has never received a decision. The good old Tudor and Stuart principles have been suffered to remain unquestioned here. Foreign politics are questions of State. Under Elizabeth and James nothing was to be inquired into, nothing was to be known; everything was matter of State. On other points the veil has been torn away;

but with regard to these, there has been a sort of tacit understanding between Ministers and people.

Hitherto war has been the national rage; peace has always come too soon, war too late. To tie up the Ministers' hands and make them continually accountable would be depriving them of numberless occasions of seizing those happy advantages that lead to war; it would be lessening the people's chance of their favourite amusement. For these hundred years past Ministers, to do them justice, have generally been more backward than the people; the great object has rather been to force them into the war than to keep them out of it. Walpole and Newcastle were both forced into war.

It admits of no doubt, if we are really for war, and fond of it for its own sake, we can do no better than let things continue as they are. If we think peace better than war, it is equally certain that the law of secrecy cannot be too soon abolished.

Such is the general confusion of ideas, such the power of the imagination, such the force of prejudice, that I verily believe the persuasion is not an uncommon one. So clear in their notions are many worthy gentlemen that they look upon war, if successful, as a cause of opulence and prosperity. With equal justice might they look upon the loss of a leg as a cause of swiftness.

Well, but if it be not directly the cause of opulence, it is indirectly. From the successes of war come, say they, our prosperity, our greatness. Thence the respect paid to us by Foreign Powers; thence our security. And who does not know how necessary security is to opulence?

No, war is, in this way, just as unfavourable to opulence as in the other. In the present mode of carrying on war—a mode which it is in no man's power to depart from—security is in proportion to opulence. Just so far then as war is, by its direct effects, unfavourable to opulence, just so far is it unfavourable to security.

Respect is a term I shall beg leave to change; respect is a mixture of fear and esteem, but for constituting esteem force is not the instrument, but justice. The sentiment really relied upon for security is fear. By respect then is meant, in plain English, fear. But in a case like this fear is much more adverse

than favourable to security. So many as fear you join against
you till they think they are too strong for you, and then they
are afraid of you no longer.   Meantime they all hate you, and
jointly and severally they do you as much mischief as they
can. You, on your part, are not behindhand with them. Conscious or not conscious of your own bad intentions, you suspect
theirs to be still worse. Their notion of your intentions is the
same. Measures of mere self-defence are naturally taken for
projects of aggression. The same causes produce, on both sides,
the same effects; each makes haste to begin for fear of being
forestalled. In this state of things, if on either side there happen
to be a Minister, or a would-be Minister, who has a fancy for
war, the stroke is struck, and the tinder catches fire.

At school the strongest boy may perhaps be the safest. Two
or more boys are not always in readiness to join against one.
But though this notion may hold good in an English school, it
will not bear transplanting upon the theatre of Europe.

Oh! But if your neighbours are really afraid of you, their fear
is of use to you in another way; you get the turn of the scale
in all disputes. Points that are at all doubtful they give up to
you of course. Watch the moment, and you may every now
and then gain points that do not admit of doubt. This is only
the former old set of fallacies exhibited in a more obscure form,
and which, from their obscurity only, can show as new. The
fact is, as has been already shown, there is no nation that has
any points to gain to the prejudice of any other. Between the
interests of nations there is nowhere any real conflict; if they
appear repugnant anywhere, it is only in proportion as they
are misunderstood. What are these points? What points are
these which, if you had your choice, you would wish to gain
of them? Preferences in trade have been proved to be worth
nothing; distant territorial acquisitions have been proved to be
worth less than nothing. When these are out of the question,
what other points are there worth gaining by such means.

Opulence is the word I have first mentioned, but opulence
is not the word that would be first pitched upon. The repugnancy of the connection between war and opulence is too glaring;
the term " opulence " brings to view an idea too simple, too
intelligible, too precise. Splendour, greatness, glory, these are

terms better suited to the purpose. Prove first that war contributes to splendour and greatness, you may persuade yourself
it contributes to opulence, because when you think of splendour
you think of opulence. But splendour, greatness, glory, all these
fine things, may be produced by useless success, and unprofitable
and enervating extent of dominion obtained at the expense of
opulence; and this is the way in which you may manage so as
to prove to yourself that the way to make a man run the quicker
is to cut off one of his legs. And true enough it is that a man
who has had a leg cut off, and the stump healed, may hop
faster than a man who lies in bed with both legs broken can
walk; and thus you may prove that Britain is in a better
case after the expenditure of a glorious war than if there had
been no war, because France or some other country was put by
it into a still worse condition.

In respect, therefore, of any benefit to be derived in the
shape of conquest or of trade, of opulence or of respect, no
advantage can be reaped by the employment of the unnecessary,
the mischievous, and unconstitutional system of clandestinity
and· secrecy in negotiation.

Printed in Great Britain by the Eastern Press, Ltd., Reading.